Kathy Schrock's
Every Day of the School Year Series

Teaching Social Studies Through Literature: Grades 4-6

by
Nancy J. Keane

LINWORTH
LEARNING

A Publication of Linworth Learning

Linworth Publishing, Inc.
Worthington, Ohio

To my children, Aureta and Alex Keane

And to the memory of my mother, Aureta C. Keane

Cataloging-in-Publication Data

Published by Linworth Publishing, Inc.
480 East Wilson Bridge Road, Suite L
Worthington, Ohio 43085

1-58683-105-4

5 4 3 2 1

❖ Table of Contents ❖

Acknowledgements

I wish to thank the people who have helped with this endeavor. First, I would like to thank all the authors who gave us these marvelous stories to enjoy. With so many children's books in print, it was quite difficult to limit the choice of entries in this book. Without these extraordinary people, this would have been an arduous task. As it is, I have spent numerous, entertaining hours wrapped up in the books.

I would also like to thank the many librarians I have come in contact with. They have introduced me to books I may have missed. The library staff of the Concord (NH) School District has been very helpful, especially when I begged to borrow books from their collections. The staff of the Children's Room at Concord (NH) Public Library also has been helpful. Their fantastic collection kept me ensconced in quality literature for many days. They were particularly generous in retrieving books for me during their renovation when the books were not accessible to the public.

The many wonderful, dedicated teachers I have had the privilege of knowing also influenced this work tremendously. Their ideas for activities and their willingness to share helped a great deal. I have been very fortunate to work with a talented group of educators. Thanks also to Kathy Schrock for her support of this work. She has gone above and beyond.

Most importantly, I would like to thank my family. My children, Aureta and Alex, didn't complain too much about the amount of time I spent in the library or on the computer. They listened to the books I read to them and gave me their opinions. They understood when I would start booktalking a new book at seemingly random times. If you really want to know if a child will like a book, ask a child. My children are the best!

How to Use This Book

$\mathcal{U}$sing children's literature in the classroom to introduce or extend a lesson is a proven way to get students involved in the subject. Using children's literature to expand social studies curriculum is becoming more and more popular. Information presented in a story form is accessible to kids and can be used as a jumping off point to effectively introduce a specific social studies topic.

This book contains lesson ideas, booktalks and recommended book titles which center on social studies themes. These are all based on children's literature that works well with the theme. The suggested book lists include books that reflect the theme of the chapter. The information given for each book includes the author, title, publisher, date of publication, interest level (IL-given as grade level) and reading level (RL-given as grade level). In addition, a short annotation based on the Library of Congress summary statement is included.

Activities are tied in with each theme and the related book recommendations. These activities are samples and ideas of the type of things you may want to do with your students in order to follow up and expand upon a theme. They are just starter activities and leave plenty of room for you to personalize the activity for your students. By introducing a concept via fiction, the door is thrown open to expand the exploration of the topic in more depth.

Standards-based curriculum holds a great potential for student achievement. For over a decade, the Mid-Continent Research for Education and Learning Group (McREL) has been a recognized leader in developing K-12 standards. Throughout this book, the McREL standards are referenced at the beginning of each chapter. McREL standards can be accessed at http://www.mcrel.org. Additionally, reference is made when appropriate to the International Society for Technology in Education (ITSE) National Educational Technology Standards (NETS). These standards can be viewed at http://www.cnets.iste.org.

The purpose of this book is to promote fiction reading and to get students excited about social studies curriculum. One way to excite children about reading and gathering information is to use booktalks as hooks. Booktalks are short book promotions that tease the student into wanting to know more. When children hear about books through friends' recommendations or through booktalks, they are more apt to read the book themselves. The booktalks presented here can serve as a starting point for further discovery and can lead into the related activities.

After giving a booktalk yourself, choose a book under one of the topic areas and assign a group of students to read the book. Then have them work together to give a booktalk in front of the class. The goal is to interest other students in reading the book and to stimulate a discussion on the topic. Students are often drawn towards fiction for their reading choices. By using fiction as a springboard for learning, children will be able to connect reading for pleasure and reading for information.

Author's note: To find out more about booktalking and to access a database of ready-to-use booktalks, visit the author's Web page *Booktalks—Quick and Simple* at http://www.nancykeane.com. The author has also set up a listserv to share and discuss booktalks. To join, simply visit the Web site and click on "Join Booktalkers Group" or go to http://groups.yahoo.com/group/booktalkers/

About the Author

Nancy J. Keane is a school librarian in Concord, New Hampshire. She has been a lover of children's literature all her life, so working with books and children is a perfect match for her. In addition to her work in the school, Nancy also hosts a radio show on WKXL radio in Concord. *Kids Book Beat* is a monthly show that features children from the area booktalking about their favorite books. The show is live and very unpredictable! Nancy also has authored a children's fiction book and several books on using booktalks.

Nancy is the author of an award-winning Web site, *Booktalks—Quick and Simple*, at <http://www.nancykeane.com/booktalks/>. The site logs about 500 hits a day and has proven to be indispensable to librarians and teachers. The database includes more than 1,100 ready-to-use booktalks and welcomes contributions from educators. Additionally, Nancy has set up a listserv to bring together people who want to discuss booktalking and share booktalks. This list welcomes new members and may be joined by contacting *booktalkers@yahoogroups.com*.

Nancy received a B.A. from the University of Massachusetts, Amherst, an M.L.S. from the University of Rhode Island, and an M.A. in Educational Technology from George Washington University. She is an adjunct faculty member at New Hampshire Technical College, Connected University, and she teaches workshops for the University of New Hampshire.

Nancy lives in Concord, New Hampshire, with her children, Aureta and Alex. They share their home with their dog and four cats.

A Word From
❖ Kathy Schrock ❖

*W*elcome to the Every Day of the School Year Series. As an educator, library media specialist, and now technology administrator, I know how important it is for the classroom teacher to extend the learning experiences in the classroom. With the current focus on standards-based teaching, learning, and assessment, I felt it was important to supply classroom teachers and library media specialists with activities that directly support the curriculum, but at the same time allow for creative teachers to supplement and extend activities for their students.

The activities in this series are varied in scope, but all of them provide practical tips, tricks, ideas, activities and units. Many of the activities include related print and Internet sites that are easily collected by the classroom teacher before engaging in the activity. There are handouts, worksheets, and much more throughout the books, too.

In my job as technology administrator for a school district, I am often able to plan lessons with teachers and visit classrooms to observe the teaching of the lesson. In addition, as the creator and maintainer, since 1995, of Kathy Schrock's Guide for Educators (http://discoveryschool.com/schrockguide/), a portal of categorized Web sites for teachers, I often receive e-mail from teachers who are searching for practical, creative, and easy-to-implement activities for the classroom. I hope this series provides just the impetus for you to stretch and enhance your textbook, lesson, and standards-based unit by use of these activities.

If you have any titles you would like to see added to the series, or would like to author yourself, drop me a note at kathy@kathyschrock.net

Kathy Schrock

American Revolution

Introduction:

Stars and stripes. Fireworks and parades. These are the symbols of America's freedom. Back in 1776, America was a colony of England and then independence was declared. The Colonies would become a separate country but not before years of war and turmoil. This chapter includes books that tell of America's struggle for independence and the men and women who worked to achieve it. The activities help illustrate the importance of maintaining our independence and strength.

United States History
Era 3 – Revolution and the New Nation (1754–1820s)

Standard 6
Understands the causes of the American Revolution, the ideas and interests involved in shaping the revolutionary movement, and reasons for the American victory

Level II Grade: 5–6

2. Understands the events that contributed to the outbreak of the American Revolution and the earliest armed conflict of the Revolutionary War (e.g., opponents and defenders of England's new imperial policy, the idea of "taxation without representation," the battle at Lexington and Concord)

4. Understands the major developments and chronology of the Revolutionary War and the roles of its political, military, and diplomatic leaders (e.g., George Washington, Benjamin Franklin, Thomas Jefferson, John Adams, Samuel Adams, John Hancock, Richard Henry Lee)

5. Understands perspectives of and the roles played in the American Revolution by various groups of people (e.g., men, women, white settlers, free and enslaved African-Americans, and Native Americans)

Standards Addressed (NETS)

Performance Indicators For Technology-Literate Students

GRADES 3–5

4. Use general purpose productivity tools and peripherals to support personal productivity, remediate skill deficits, and facilitate learning throughout the curriculum.

5. Use technology tools (e.g., multimedia authoring, presentation, Web tools, digital cameras, scanners) for individual and collaborative writing, communication, and publishing activities to create knowledge products for audiences inside and outside the classroom.

6. Use telecommunications efficiently to access remote information, communicate with others in support of direct and independent learning, and pursue personal interests.

Sample Booktalk:

Berleth, Richard. *Samuel's Choice*. Chicago: Albert Whitman, 1990. IL 3-6, RL 5.2

The year is 1776 and 14-year-old Samuel is a slave on a farm in Brooklyn. Samuel has been separated from his family and friends and hopes that one day he may be free to go where he wants and see whom he wants. There is talk of severing ties with England and Samuel hopes that they may help him in some way. When the Declaration of Independence is posted near the farm, Samuel's owner tears it down and Samuel wonders if the word liberty is meant only for the colonists and not for Africans. When the fighting reaches Brooklyn, Samuel uses his owner's boat to rescue many American soldiers. One of the soldiers turns out to be Major Mordecai Gist who asks Samuel to join the Americans as a boatman for General George Washington. The war has just become very important to Samuel and his future. Join Samuel as he goes from slave to hero in SAMUEL'S CHOICE.

Booklist:

Banim, Lisa. *Drums at Saratoga*. New York: Silver Moon/August House, c1993, IL 3-6, RL 5.1
Lured by the glamour and excitement of a soldier's life, 11-year-old Nathaniel follows the British army down the Hudson Valley during the American Revolution and witnesses the true hardships of war firsthand.

Banim, Lisa. *A Spy In The King's Colony*. New York: Silver Moon, 1994, IL 3-6, RL 5.3
In British-occupied Boston in 1776, 11-year-old Emily Parker is determined to find out if a family friend is a traitor to the American patriots.

Borden, Louise. *Sleds On Boston Common: A Story From The American Revolution*. New York: M. K. McElderry Books, c2000, IL 3-6, RL 5.8
Henry complains to the royal governor, General Gage, after his plan to sled down the steep hill at Boston Common is thwarted by the masses of British troops camped there.

Duey, Kathleen. *Mary Alice Peale, Philadelphia, 1777*. New York: Aladdin Paperbacks, 1996, IL 3-6, RL 3.5
When her wounded brother returns from battle, 12-year-old Mary must get help for him without telling her father, a wealthy Tory, who has disowned his son for joining General Washington's Continental Army.

Durrant, Lynda. *Betsy Zane: The Rose Of Fort Henry*. New York: Clarion Books, c2000, IL 5-8, RL 5.7
In 1781, 12-year-old Elizabeth Zane, great-great-aunt of novelist Zane Grey, leaves Philadelphia to return to her brothers' homestead near Fort Henry in what is now West Virginia, where she plays an important role in the final battle of the American Revolution.

Forbes, Esther. *Johnny Tremain*. Boston: Houghton Mifflin, c1971., IL 5-8, RL 5.3
After injuring his hand, a silversmith's apprentice in Boston becomes a messenger for the Sons of Liberty in the days before the American Revolution.

Gregory, Kristiana. *Five Smooth Stones: Hope's Diary*. New York: Scholastic, 2001, IL 3-6, RL 4.6
In her diary, a young girl writes about her life and the events surrounding the beginning of the American Revolution in Philadelphia in 1776.

Hedstrom, Deborah. *From Colonies To Country With George Washington*. Sisters, Or: Questar, 1997, IL 3-6, RL 4.5
A fictionalized account of the Revolutionary War, told from the point of view of an aide to George Washington.

Moss, Marissa. *Emma's Journal: The Story Of A Colonial Girl*. San Diego: Silver Whistle/Harcourt Brace, c1999, IL 3-6, RL 4.6
From 1774 to 1776, Emma describes in her journal her stay in Boston, where she witnesses the British blockade and spies for the American militia. Features hand-printed text, drawings, and marginal notes.

Reit, Seymour. *Guns For General Washington: A Story Of The American Revolution.* San Diego: Harcourt Brace, c1990, IL 5-8, RL 5.8
Frustrated with life under siege in George Washington's army, 19-year-old Will Knox and his brother Colonel Henry Knox undertake the task of moving 183 cannons from Fort Ticonderoga to Boston in the dead of winter.

Suggested Activities:

Activity# 1: Silversmiths

One of the leaders of the American independence movement was a silversmith by the name of Paul Revere. Caught up in the fervor of the times, it was Paul Revere who set out on his horse to warn the farmers in Massachusetts that the "British are coming!" After learning about Paul Revere and his silversmithing, students will become amateur silversmiths. Students can sculpt bowls or platters with aluminum foil and display their creations at a colonial fair in the classroom.

Activity# 2: Revolutionary Broadside

During the time of the Revolution, there was no television or radio or even computers for the people to use to share information. One common way for people to let people know what was going on was to create a broadside. A broadside would be in the form of a poster that would be hung up around town to tell the citizens what was going on. Have students create a broadside explaining the revolt. This should be a broadside that may have been posted during the time of the revolution. Students need to remember they want to be sure to entice others to join their cause.

Activity# 3: Mapping the Revolution

Have students create a map of the American Revolution. Students should mark significant events on the map. These can include the Boston Tea Party, Lexington Green, etc. Students can concentrate on one state or area or include all 13 colonies. Students can also locate the home area of the characters in the books they have read.

Activity# 4: Revolutionary Trading Cards

There were many heroes of the American Revolution. There were the military and political leaders, the farmers, and the brave women. Have each student research one person who took part in the Revolution. Have students create trading cards with information about that person. One side of the card should include a picture that can be found on the Internet, an electronic encyclopedia, scanned from a book or drawn by the student. Make sure the citation to the source of the photo is included on the card! The other side could include birth and death dates, a brief family history, role in the Revolution and other miscellaneous facts about the person. These can be used to build a classroom set of informational trading cards. See Handout #1: *Revolutionary Trading Cards.*

Handout #1: Revolutionary Trading Cards

Front of card should include a picture of the person and the name

Name:

Lived:

Role in Revolution:

Family:

Interesting facts:

Back of the card should include information about the person

Front of card should include a picture of the person and the name

Name:

Lived:

Role in Revolution:

Family:

Interesting facts:

Back of the card should include information about the person

Activity# 5: **Real American Heros**

There were many heroes of the American Revolution. Ordinary people were put in extraordinary situations. These ordinary people often rose to the challenge and performed in ways they never dreamed. In this activity, students will research a major American Revolutionary War hero and become that person.

■ Students will be given the name of a person who was important during the Revolution.

■ Students will research that person and note important facts about him/her.

> ► Birth date
> ► Occupation
> ► Family
> ► Role in the Revolution

■ Student will create a costume to represent their person.

■ Student will present a first-person account of their life and role during the American Revolution.

Some useful URLs include:

History Place
http://www.historyplace.com/unitedstates/revolution/index.html

18th Century Clothing in Colonial Williamsburg
http://www.colonialwilliamsburg.com/Almanack/life/clothing/home.html

❖ Ancient Civilizations ❖

Introduction:

We all seem to have a fascination with the ancient world, from mummies and chariot races to gladiators and pharaohs. In this chapter, we'll take a journey back in time to visit some of the ancient places the students can learn about. We'll learn about what life was like for people all those many years ago. The books we will read tell the stories in a way that can be understood by children of the 21st century. The activities will give the students a bit more understanding of life in the ancient world. Ready? Let's turn back the hands of time.

Standards Addressed (McREL)
World History
Era 2 – Early Civilizations and the Rise of Pastoral Peoples, 4000–1000 BCE

Standard 4
Understands how agrarian societies spread and new states emerged in the third and second millennia BCE

Level II Grade: 5-6

3. Understands the role of technology in early agrarian societies (e.g., how the advent of the plow influenced new agrarian societies in Southwest Asia, the Mediterranean basin, and temperate Europe; how megalithic stone buildings, such as Stonehenge, indicate the emergence of complex agrarian societies in Europe; changes for humankind and civilization brought on by the bow and arrow and by pottery; what physical evidence indicated about the characteristics of the agrarian society of ancient Egypt and the life of the Pharaoh)

World History Across the Eras

Standard 46
Understands long-term changes and recurring patterns in world history

Level II Grade: 5-6

2. Understands major patterns of long-distance trade from ancient times to the present and how trade has contributed to economic and cultural change in particular societies or civilizations

Standards Addressed (NETS)
Performance Indicators For Technology-Literate Students

Grades 3-5

4. Use general purpose productivity tools and peripherals to support personal productivity, remediate skill deficits, and facilitate learning throughout the curriculum.

5. Use technology tools (e.g., multimedia authoring, presentation, Web tools, digital cameras, scanners) for individual and collaborative writing, communication, and publishing activities to create knowledge products for audiences inside and outside the classroom.

6. Use telecommunications efficiently to access remote information, communicate with others in support of direct and independent learning, and pursue personal interests.

Sample Booktalk:

Carter, Dorothy Sharp. *His Majesty, Queen Hatshepsut.* New York: Lippincott, 1987. IL 5-8, RL 6.4

So, what do you think you know about how people who lived back in ancient Egypt? What types of things are found in the tombs of the great kings? What does this tell about their lives and their family? This is the story of a young girl living in Ancient Egypt who doesn't want to live the way that everyone expects her to. She knows girls can never be King so she cannot follow in her father's footsteps. She is forced to marry her brother so the power will stay in the family. But she is no ordinary woman. When her husband dies, she declares herself to be a man and starts wearing men's clothing and even a snap-on beard. She rules her kingdom as she sees fit. All her life she has been told how fortunate she is to be born of royalty. She has never felt fortunate. But, at last, as she takes her life into her own hands, she does find happiness and love. All the while, her son is plotting against her so that he can ascend to the throne. This is a story of what life may have been like for those who lived so long ago. Come with us to ancient Egypt in HIS MAJESTY, QUEEN HATSHEPSUT.

Booklist:

Bailey, Linda. *Adventures In Ancient Egypt.* Toronto; Niagara Falls, NY: Kids Can Press, c2000, IL 3-6, RL 5.4
The three Binkerton children pay a visit to the Good Times Travel Agency and find themselves living in ancient Egypt where it is "tough and scary," "hot and sweaty" and "fun."

Bunting, Eve. *I Am The Mummy Heb-Nefert.* San Diego: Harcourt Brace & Co, c1997, IL 3-6, RL 4.2
A mummy recalls her past life in ancient Egypt as the beautiful wife of the Pharaoh's brother.

Galloway, Priscilla. *Aleta And The Queen: A Tale Of Ancient Greece.* New York: Annick Press, Distributed in the U.S.A. by Firefly Books, c1995, IL 3-6, RL 6.2
When her husband Odysseus leaves to fight at Troy, Queen Penelope is left to rule Ithaca for 19 years.

Heide, Florence Parry. *The House of Wisdom.* New York: DK, c1999, IL 3-6, RL 7.0
Ishaq, the son of the chief translator to the Caliph of ancient Baghdad, travels the world in search of precious books and manuscripts and brings them back to the great library known as the House of Wisdom.

Korman, Gordon. *Your Mummy Is A Nose Picker.* New York: Hyperion Books for Children, c2000, IL 3-6, RL 5.2
Devin and his alien visitor Stan from the planet Pan travel back to ancient Egypt in search of Nile Delta goldenrod which will save Stan's job by ensuring that all Pan tourists on Earth sneeze.

Macaulay, David. *Rome Antics.* Boston: Houghton Mifflin, 1997, IL 3-6, RL 5.5
A pigeon carrying an important message takes the reader on a unique tour which includes both ancient and modern parts of the city of Rome.

Osborne, Mary Pope. *Day of the Dragon King.* New York: Random House, c1998, IL 3-6, RL 2.2
The magic tree house takes Jack and Annie back 2,000 years to ancient China where they must find the original copy of an old legend before the Imperial Library is burned down by the evil Dragon King.

Rubalcaba, Jill. *A Place In The Sun*. New York: Clarion Books, c1997, IL 3-6, RL 4.2
In ancient Egypt, the gifted young son of a sculptor is taken into slavery when he attempts to save his father's life, and is himself almost killed before his exceptional talent leads Pharoah to name him Royal Sculptor.

Scieszka, Jon. *See You Later, Gladiator*. New York: Viking, c2000, IL 3-6, RL 4.8
Joe, Fred, and Sam demonstrate some of their favorite professional wrestling moves, including the "Time Warp Trio Blind Ninja Smackdown," when they're transported to ancient Rome and forced to fight as gladiators in the Colosseum.

Scieszka, Jon. *Tut, Tut*. New York: Viking, c1996, IL 3-6, RL 3.5
Sam, Joe, and Fred finish their school project on ancient Egypt without using their magical time travel book, but when Joe's sister Anna plays with it and travels to the land of pyramids, they must follow her back in time to bring her back to 1996.

Suggested Activities:

Activity #1: Archaeologist of the Future

Imagine that you are an archaeologist living 1,000 years from now. You have just come upon a very well-preserved structure that you believe dates back to the year 2002 in a place named the United States. What might you find when you dig up the artifacts? What might you decide the artifacts were used for?

Activity #2: Time Capsule

What would you like people of the future to know about you, your school, and your town? Create a time capsule with information that you think will be of interest to people in the future. Each student should fill out an index card with his or her "fact." If you have access to a place to bury the time capsule, you can designate a time when it should be dug up. It would be fun to have a time capsule that is to be opened when the students graduate from high school.

Activity #3: Ancient Civilization Trivia

Have students prepare an ancient civilization trivia game. Each student will come up with a question and answer for information that is known about the ancient world. These can be written on index cards. Students can compete individually or in groups.

Activity #4: You Can Take It With You

Introduce the students to Egyptian pyramids. These were burial chambers for very important people. The pharaohs and their families were buried along with items that were considered important for their journey ahead in the afterlife. Find out what types of objects were buried along with the person. What was their significance? If you were creating a monument to a leader today, what objects would you bury with that person? What is the significance of those items? Students can find information about what was found in some pyramids at Virtual Egypt. http://www.virtual-egypt.com/newhtml/mummies

Activity #5: **The First Olympics**

The very first Olympic games took place in ancient times in the year 776 B.C. There were no television networks scrambling over the rights to air the games. There were no cities vying to host them. There were no squabbles about what events to hold where. There was a set place and set events. Students will research the first Olympic games and report on the events.

You have been hired as a sports reporter for ESPN. Your assignment is to cover the Olympics in the year 776. This is the first time the games are being held and your audience isn't really sure why the games are happening or what they will be seeing. It is your job to explain why the games are held and then give an account of the events. Write a script for your report. Be sure to include:

■ Background information on the reason the games are held

■ Who is participating and from what countries or locations

■ Pre-game ceremony information

■ List of events

■ Description of events and winners.

❖ Civil War ❖

Introduction:

Brother against brother and father against son. The American Civil War was a very hard time in the history of the United States. Why did our country go to war with itself? What were some of the consequences? In this chapter, we will look at some novels that deal with the Civil War. The activities will help to extend the students' knowledge of that period.

Standards Addressed (McREL)
United States History
Era 4 – Expansion and Reform (1801–1861)

Standard 11
Understands the extension, restriction, and reorganization of political democracy after 1800

Level II Grade: 5-6

3. Understands divisive issues prior to the Civil War (e.g., the Missouri Compromise and its role in determining slave and non-slave land areas, the issues that divided the North and the South)

Era 5 – Civil War and Reconstruction (1850–1877)

Standard 13
Understands the causes of the Civil War

Level II Grade: 5-6

1. Understands slavery prior to the Civil War (e.g., the importance of slavery as a principal cause of the Civil War, the growing influence of abolitionists, children's roles and family life under slavery)

2. Knows the locations of the southern and northern states and their economic resources (e.g., the industries and small family farms of the industrial North, the agricultural economy and slavery of the South)

Standard 14
Understands the course and character of the Civil War and its effects on the American people

Level II Grade: 5-6

1. Understands the technological, social, and strategic aspects of the Civil War (e.g., the impact of innovations in military technology; turning points of the war; leaders of the Confederacy and Union; conditions, characteristics, and armies of the Confederacy and Union; major areas of Civil War combat)

2. Understands the provisions and significance of the Emancipation Proclamation (e.g., reasons Abraham Lincoln issued it, public reactions to it in the North and the South)

3. Understands the impact of the Civil War on social and gender issues (e.g., the roles of women on the home front and on the battlefield; the human and material costs of the war; the degree to which the war united the nation; how it changed the lives of women, men, and children)

Standards Addressed (NETS)
Performance Indicators For Technology—Literate Students

Grades 3–5

4. Use general purpose productivity tools and peripherals to support personal productivity, remediate skill deficits, and facilitate learning throughout the curriculum.

5. Use technology tools (e.g., multimedia authoring, presentation, Web tools, digital cameras, scanners) for individual and collaborative writing, communication, and publishing activities to create knowledge products for audiences inside and outside the classroom.

6. Use telecommunications efficiently to access remote information, communicate with others in support of direct and independent learning, and pursue personal interests.

Sample Booktalk:

Hunt, Irene. *Across Five Aprils.* New York: Silver Burdett, 1992. IL 5-8 RL 6.6

Young Jethro Creighton watches the beginnings of the Civil War. He has older brothers on opposite sides of the dispute. His idol, the schoolteacher engaged to his sister, also joins the fight. Jethro is left at home to do the work formerly shared by all the brothers. In ACROSS FIVE APRILS, we relive Jethro's aching muscles and fearful rides back from town for supplies. We also witness the boy's innocent faith in the Presidency and his brave defense of a cousin who deserted.

Booklist:

Brill, Marlene Targ. *Diary Of A Drummer Boy.* Brookfield, Conn.: Millbrook Press, c1998, IL 3-6, RL 4.8
This is a fictionalized diary of a 12-year-old boy who joins the Union army as a drummer and ends up fighting in the Civil War.

De Angeli, Marguerite. *Thee, Hannah!* Scottdale, PA: Herald Press, 2000, c1968, IL 3-6, RL 4.7
Nine-year-old Hannah, a Quaker living in Philadelphia just before the Civil War, longs to have some fashionable dresses like other girls. However, she comes to appreciate her heritage and its plain dressing when her family saves the life of a runaway slave.

Duey, Kathleen. *Amelina Carrett: Bayou Grand Coeur, Louisiana, 1863.* New York: Aladdin Paperbacks, 1999, IL 3-6, RL 6.2
When 13-year-old Amelina saves the life of a young Yankee spy found injured near her Louisiana home in 1863, the orphaned girl creates a dangerous situation for herself and her uncle.

Garrity, Jennifer Johnson. *The Bushwhacker: A Civil War Adventure.* Atlanta: Peachtree, c1999, IL 3-6, RL 5.3
While the Civil War rages in Missouri and Rebels destroy their farm home and scatter their family, 13-year-old Jacob and his younger sister find refuge in an unlikely place.

Hall, Beverly B. *The Secret Of The Lion's Head.* Shippensburg, Pa.: White Mane Pub. Co, c1995, IL 3-6, RL 4.8
Living with her aunt in Richmond during the Civil War, Annie notices mysterious goings on and suspects that Auntie Elizabeth is a Union spy.

Love, D. Anne. *Three Against The Tide*. New York: Holiday House, c1998, IL 3-6, RL 8.2
After her father is called away from their plantation near Charleston, S.C, during the Civil War, 12-year-old Susanna must lead her brothers on a difficult journey in hopes of being reunited with their father.

Pryor, Bonnie. *Joseph: 1861— A Rumble Of War*. New York: Morrow Junior Books, c1999, IL 3-6, RL 5.3
After his stepfather becomes an abolitionist, 10-year-old Joseph struggles with his own thoughts about slavery as he sees its divisive power in his small Kentucky town.

Reeder, Carolyn. *Shades Of Gray* New York:.Simon & Schuster Books for Young Readers, c1989, IL 3-6, RL 5.5
At the end of the Civil War, 12-year-old Will, having lost all his immediate family, reluctantly leaves his city home to live in the Virginia countryside with his aunt and the uncle he considers a traitor because he refused to take part in the war.

Roop, Peter. *Grace's Letter To Lincoln*. New York: Hyperion Books for Children, c1998, IL 3-6, RL 3.4
On the eve of the 1860 presidential election, as war clouds gather and the South threatens to secede, 11-year-old Grace decides to help Abraham Lincoln get elected by writing and advising him to grow a beard.

Stolz, Mary. *A Ballad Of The Civil War*. New York: HarperCollins, c1997, IL 3-6, RL 5.8
Weary of the war, a Union lieutenant recalls his life with his twin brother on their family's Virginia plantation and the events that led them to fight on different sides in the Civil War.

Suggested Activities:

Activity #1: **Dear Diary**

Have the students write their own fictionalized diary of a character living during the Civil War. The character should be the same age as the student. The character may live in either the North or the South. Have the students include facts about the region or state where the student lives.

Activity #2: **Civil War Dictionary**

Have the students make a "Civil War Dictionary" for the class. The students should find five words that were used during the Civil War that we don't hear anymore. Some of these words will be found in the literature that is read. Words like *hardtack, sawbones* and *skedaddle* are probably unfamiliar to today's students. Have each student write and illustrate the definition. When each student has completed the assignment, the words can be combined into a class dictionary.

Activity #3: **Paper Bag Biography**

Create a paper bag biography on one important person from the Civil War. The items in the paper bag should represent the life of the person. The student should be able to explain why s/he chose that object. There should be a minimum of five objects in the bag. If the actual item cannot be obtained, have the student draw a picture of it on heavy paper stock.

Activity #4: **Follow the Drinking Gourd**

Before and during the Civil War, slaves were not allowed to learn to read or write. However, they did learn to communicate secretly with each other through their songs and their quilts. Have the students research some of the songs that were sung by the slaves and try to figure out the meanings. Some examples of words with different meanings are:

- *Heaven* or *home* meant a better life in the North

- *Jesus* or *Lord* usually referred to a conductor on the Underground Railroad

- *Chariot* meant the Underground Railroad

- *Drinking gourd* meant the Big Dipper. It was used in navigation as the slaves moved northward.

- *Judgment Day* referred to the day of escape from slavery

- As a follow-up activity, have students create their own code to be used for things in the classroom or school, such as lunchtime, recess, or band.

Activity #5: All Roads Lead to Civil War

No one event caused the Civil War. There were many events that led up to the outbreak of war. Students will look at different events and understand their role in the road to war. Students will learn about the causes of the Civil War. They will be introduced to resources that will be accessed for research.

- Students will be given a list of major pre-Civil War events. They will choose one event to research.

- Students will research the event and understand why it was important to Americans

- Students will write a summary stating why their event helped cause the Civil War.

- Some of the events include:

  - Compromise of 1820
  - Denmark Vessey's failed rebellion 1822
  - Nat Turner's rebellion in 1831
  - *The Liberator* is published in 1831
  - Compromise of 1850
  - *Uncle Tom's Cabin* published in 1852
  - Kansas-Nebraska Act, 1854
  - Dred Scott Decision 1857
  - The Lincoln Douglas Debates, 1858
  - John Brown's Raid, 1859

Students will be able to find much information about these topics in their text and in library resources. They may also want to search the internet. Two useful Internet sites include:

Encarta http://www.encarta.com
US Civil War Center, Louisiana State University: http://www.cwc.lsu.edu

✦ Colonial America ✦

Introduction:

During the 1600s, the Europeans began their trek to America. There were many reasons for these colonists to travel to an unknown country. Some came for economic reasons, some came for freedom, and some simply came for adventure. Whatever the reason, they created a new home and, unknowingly, a new country. In this chapter, we will spend time with the colonists who helped settle the United States and learn about some of the trials they faced. The activities will extend our knowledge about this time in history.

Standards Addressed (McREL)
United States History
Era 2 – Colonization and Settlement (1585–1763)

Standard 4
Understands how political, religious, and social institutions emerged in the English colonies

Level II Grade: 5-6

3. Understands Puritanism in colonial America (e.g., how Puritanism shaped New England communities, the changes in Puritanism during the 17th century, opposition to King James I, why Puritans came to America, the Puritan family structure)

4. Understands how and why family and community life differed in various regions of colonial North America (e.g., Williamsburg, Philadelphia, Boston, New York, French Quebec, Santa Fe)

Standard 5
Understands how the values and institutions of European economic life took root in the colonies and how slavery reshaped European and African life in the Americas

Level II Grade: 5-6

3. Understands elements of African slavery during the colonial period in North America (e.g., relocation of enslaved Africans to the Caribbean and North America, the slave trade and "the middle passage")

Standards Addressed (NETS)
Performance Indicators For Technology-Literate Students

Grades 3-5

4. Use general purpose productivity tools and peripherals to support personal productivity, remediate skill deficits, and facilitate learning throughout the curriculum.

5. Use technology tools (e.g., multimedia authoring, presentation, Web tools, digital cameras, scanners) for individual and collaborative writing, communication, and publishing activities to create knowledge products for audiences inside and outside the classroom.

6. Use telecommunications efficiently to access remote information, communicate with others in support of direct and independent learning, and pursue personal interests.

Sample Booktalk:

Speare, Elizabeth. *The Witch Of Blackbird Pond*. New York: Dell, 1987. IL 5-8, RL 7.4

Kit Tyler reaches the Connecticut colony in 1687 on brig Dolph from Barbados where she has grown up in style with her well-read grandfather. When she arrives in Connecticut, she lives with her aunt and cousins. Life in the new world is much harder than she is used to. She is introduced to the stark life of making flax, cornmeal and stoking fires for soap making. She befriends an old Quaker woman, Hannah Tupper, as does Nat Eaton, the captain's son. When Kit is accused of being a witch, Nat comes to her rescue, while her own fiancé ignores her need. Kit leaves with Nat as he readies his new boat and leaves her family after having successfully brought Hannah to safety and her cousin out of sickness. To get a good sense of what colonial life was like, spend some time with THE WITCH OF BLACKBIRD POND.

Booklist:

Collier, James Lincoln. *The Corn Raid*. Lincolnwood, Ill.: Jamestown Publishers, c2000, IL 5-8, RL 5.6
Richard Ayre travels to America to become an indentured servant in the Jamestown Colony, where he befriends an Indian boy who teaches him an important lesson about friendship.

Cooney, Caroline B. *The Ransom Of Mercy Carter*. New York: Delacorte Press, c2001, IL 3-6, RL 5.1
In 1704, in the English settlement of Deerfield, Massachusetts, 11-year-old Mercy, her family, and her neighbors are captured by Mohawk Indians and their French allies. They are forced to march through bitter cold to French Canada, where some adapt to new lives and some still hope to be ransomed.

Curry, Jane Louise. *A Stolen Life*. New York: M.K. McElderry, c1999, IL 5-8, RL 6.0
In 1758 in Scotland, teenaged Jamesina MacKenzie finds her courage and resolution severely tested when she is abducted by "spiriters" and, after a harrowing voyage across the Atlantic, sold as a bond slave to a Virginia planter.

Duey, Kathleen. *Sarah Anne Hartford: Massachusetts, 1651*. New York: Aladdin Paperbacks, 1996, IL 3-6, RL 4.8
Twelve-year-old Sarah breaks the Sabbath in Puritan New England and faces a moral dilemma when an innocent person is accused in her place.

Grote, JoAnn A. *Danger In The Harbor: Grain Riots Threaten Boston*. Philadelphia: Chelsea House, c1999, IL 3-6, RL 5.3
When Queen Anne's War leaves Boston with major problems, such as food shortages and riots, 10-year-old Beth and her family struggle to survive peacefully.

Harness, Cheryl. *Three Young Pilgrims*. Toronto: Bradbury Press c1992, IL 3-6, RL 5.2
Mary, Remember, and Bartholomew are among the pilgrims who survive the harsh early years in America and see New Plymouth grow into a prosperous colony.

Hermes, Patricia. *Our Strange New Land: Elizabeth's Diary*. New York: Scholastic, 2000, IL 3-6, RL 4.2
Nine-year-old Elizabeth keeps a journal of her experiences in the New World as she encounters Indians, suffers hunger and the death of friends, and helps her father build their first home.

Karwoski, Gail. *Surviving Jamestown: The Adventures of Young Sam Collier*. Atlanta: Peachtree, c2001, IL 3-6, RL 5.7
Sam Collier, a 12-year-old, serves as page to John Smith during the relentless hardship experienced by the founders at the first permanent English settlement in the New World.

Lough, Loree. *Dream Seekers: Roger Williams's Stand For Freedom*. Philadelphia: Chelsea House, c1999, IL 3-6, RL 4.7
When 12-year-old Phillip and his sister move with their parents from Plymouth to Boston in 1634, they encounter mysterious Indians and survive narrow escapes.

Lutz, Norma Jean. *Smallpox Strikes!: Cotton Mather's Bold Experiment.* Philadelphia: Chelsea House, c1999, IL 3-6, RL 6.7
When a smallpox epidemic strikes Boston in 1721, 11-year-old Rob becomes the sole caregiver of his stepfather and brother during the time of their illness.

Osborne, Mary Pope. *Standing In The Light: The Captive Diary Of Catherine Carey Logan.* New York: Scholastic, c1998, IL 5-8, RL 4.8
A Quaker girl's diary reflects her experiences growing up in the Delaware River Valley of Pennsylvania and her capture by Lenape Indians in 1763.

Suggested Activities:

Activity #1: Dear Character

Have students write a letter to a character in the book. Let them know how similar or different they are from you. Tell them what you admire about them. What would you like to know more about them or their lives?

Activity #1: Candles

Have students make candles as the Colonists did. To find instructions, visit http://www.candleteacher.com/

Activity #3: A Day in the Life

Visit Colonial Williamsburg site: http://www.history.org
Visit Plimoth Plantation site: http://www.plimoth.org

Students will write a diary entry of what a typical day might be like in each. How are they similar? How are they different?

Activity #4: Charting History

The underlying reasons for the settlements in New England were different from those in the South. Have students create a chart showing the differences.

Activity #5: Colonial Villages

The villages that were created by the settlers in the New World reflected their reasons for coming to America as well as the environment of their surroundings. In this activity, students will create a three-dimensional colonial village. They will be able to say whether it would have been found in the North or the South. Discuss the differences between the New England settlements and the Southern settlements. How were they similar? How were they different?

The students will construct a three-dimensional model of a colonial village. They will have an understanding of why the New England or Southern Colonies were settled where they were. Students will give oral presentations explaining why their village looks as it does.

Frontier and Pioneer Life

Introduction:

As the eastern part of the United States started to become crowded, many people longed for wide-open spaces where they could spread out. The lure of the prairies and the financial enticements of the gold discoveries out West sent many people packing and looking for a new life. These pioneers packed up what they could and said goodbye to their lives in the civilized east. They often brought their families in hopes of finding a new home. These families traveled with other families in large wagon trains. Sometimes families set out on their own but they usually did not get far. What awaited them at the end of their journey? What would life be like on the frontier? Climb aboard a Conestoga wagon and hit the trail with us.

Standards Addressed (McREL)
United States History

Standard 9
Understands the United States territorial expansion between 1801 and 1861, and how it affected relations with external powers and Native Americans

Level II Grade: 5-6

5. Understands the origins of Manifest Destiny and its influence on the westward expansion of the United States (e.g., its role in the resolution of the Oregon dispute with Great Britain, how it led to the Mexican-American war)

Standard 10
Understands how the industrial revolution, increasing immigration, the rapid expansion of slavery, and the westward movement changed American lives and led to regional tensions

Level II Grade: 5-6

1. Understands the lives of immigrants in American society during the antebellum period (e.g., factors that led to increased immigration from China, Ireland, and Germany; how immigrants adapted to life in the United States and to hostility from the nativist movement and the "Know-Nothing" party)

2. Understands the major technological developments that influenced land and water transportation, the economy, international markets, and the environment between 1801 and 1860 (e.g., the importance of the spinning jenny, steam locomotive, and telegraph; the development of the canal system after 1825 and railroad system after 1860)

3. Understands social and economic elements of urban and rural life in the early and mid-19th centuries (e.g., the impact of the factory system on gender roles and the daily life of men, women, and children; factors that caused rapid urbanization; city life in the 1840s; differences in urban and rural childrens' lives, life in New England mill towns in the early 1800s, the impact of the canal and railroad on the locations and size of cities after 1820)

6. Understands elements of early western migration (e.g., the lure of the West and the reality of life on the frontier; motivations of various settlers; Mormon contributions to the settlement of the West; differences in the settlement of California and Oregon in the late 1840s and 1850s; routes taken by settlers of the Western U.S.; interactions between settlers and Native Americans and Mexicans in the western territories)

Standards Addressed (NETS)
Performance Indicators For Technology-Literate Students

Grades 3–5

4. Use general purpose productivity tools and peripherals to support personal productivity, remediate skill deficits, and facilitate learning throughout the curriculum.

5. Use technology tools (e.g., multimedia authoring, presentation, Web tools, digital cameras, scanners) for individual and collaborative writing, communication, and publishing activities to create knowledge products for audiences inside and outside the classroom.

6. Use telecommunications efficiently to access remote information, communicate with others in support of direct and independent learning, and pursue personal interests.

Sample Booktalk:

Hahn, Mary Downing. *The Gentleman Outlaw And Me—Eli: A Story Of The Old West* New York: Clarion Books, 1996. IL 5-8, RL 4.6

Twelve-year-old Eliza Yates wants to join her father in the silver mines of Colorado. Her mother has died and she is left with unfriendly relatives in Kansas. She decides to run away to find her father. Along the way, she decides that it will be easier to travel if she were a boy. She cuts off her hair, puts on overalls and a hat, and begins to call herself Eli. She soon meets up with Calvin Featherbone who calls himself Gentleman Outlaw. Calvin is off to Colorado to avenge his own father's death at the hands of Sheriff Alfred Yates, Eliza's father! The adventures these two share along the way are truly funny. Calvin is always cooking up schemes that are doomed from the start. If you enjoy funny stories with an Old West setting, THE GENTLEMAN OUTLAW AND ME—ELI will sure to entertain.

Booklist:

Antle, Nancy. *Beautiful Land: A Story Of The Oklahoma Land Rush*. New York: Puffin, 1997, IL 3-6, RL 4.5
After a two-year wait during which her mother died, 12-year-old Annie Mae and her family join 1,000s of hopeful settlers as they race to claim land in the newly-opened Oklahoma Territory.

Gregory, Kristiana. *Jenny of the Tetons*. San Diego: Harcourt Brace & Co, c1989, IL 3-6, RL 6.9
Orphaned by an Indian raid while traveling West with a wagon train, 15-year-old Carrie Hill is befriended by the English trapper Beaver Dick and taken to live with his Indian wife Jenny and their six children.

Hermes, Patricia. *Calling Me Home*. New York: Avon Camelot, c1998, IL 3-6, RL 6.9
Twelve-year-old Abbie struggles to accept her father's desire to make a new home for his family on the Nebraska prairies in the late 1850s.

Kurtz, Jane. *I'm Sorry, Almira Ann*. New York: H. Holt, 1999, IL 3-6, RL 3.0
Eight-year-old Sarah's high spirits help make her family's long journey from Missouri to Oregon more bearable, though they do cause both her and her best friend Almira Ann some problems.

Little, Jean. *The Belonging Place*. New York: Viking, 1997, IL 3-6, RL 3.5
Elspet Mary is happy to be living with her kind aunt and uncle after her mother and father die, but worries when the family decides to go from Scotland to Upper Canada to own their own farm.

Love, D. Anne. *Bess's Log Cabin Quilt*. New York: Holiday House, c1995, IL 3-6, RL 4.8
With her father away and her mother ill with fever, 10-year-old Bess works hard on a log cabin quilt to save the family farm.

Love, D. Anne. *A Year Without Rain*. New York: Holiday House, c2000, IL 3-6, RL 5.6
Her mother's death and a year-long drought has made life difficult for 12-year-old Rachel and her family on their farm in the Dakotas. When she learns that her father plans to get married again, it is almost more than Rachel can bear.

MacLachlan, Patricia. *Sarah, Plain And Tall*. New York: Charlotte Zolotow Book, c1985, IL 3-6, RL 4.2
When their father invites a mail-order bride to come live with them in their prairie home, Caleb and Anna are captivated by their new mother and hope she will stay.

Moss, Marissa. *Rachel's Journal: The Story Of A Pioneer Girl*. San Diego: Silver Whistle/Harcourt Brace, c1998, IL 3-6, RL 5.2
In this journal, Rachel chronicles her family's adventures traveling by covered wagon on the Oregon Trail in 1850.

Wallace, Bill. *Red Dog*. New York: Holiday House, c1987, IL 3-6, RL 5.8
Living with his family in the rugged and dangerous Wyoming mountains in the 1860s, 12-year-old Adam finds his courage put to the test when he is left in charge of the household during his stepfather's absence.

Suggested Activities:

Activity #1: **Frontier Games**

Life for children on the frontier was not all work. They also got together and enjoyed playing games. Have the children research what games were played by pioneer children. Organize a pioneer games day and have students participate. You can invite other classes if you would like.

Activity #2: **Quilt**

A staple for any family on the prairie was the quilt. It served the family in more ways than just to keep them warm. Women would often stitch their family stories into the quilts. If there were other women around, they would get together for quilting bees that were a common way to socialize. Create a class quilt that tells the story of your class. The quilt can be made of paper or cloth. Each student should get a 9" by 9" square or paper or cloth. The students should draw a scene representing a story about their class or school. The quilt can be joined together and displayed as a class quilt.

Activity #3: **Pioneer Letters Home**

Discuss what the life of a typical pioneer might be like. What types of people went west? What were their reasons? Why types of jobs did they do? How did they travel? What did they eat along the way? What did they wear? What kinds of homes did they build once they settled? How did they furnish their homes?

Students will take on the role of a pioneer. They will write a letter to a relative who was left back East. They will describe their journey and their new home. They should include information about their new home, their furniture, what they eat, what their daily life is like and how they feel about their new lives.

Activity #4: **Frontier Chow**

There were no microwave ovens and fast food on the prairie. Research what types of foods were eaten by the pioneers and how they were prepared. Create a class recipe book! See Handout #2: *Recipe Cards*

Activity #5: **Pioneer Scrapbook**

Often, pioneers kept scrapbooks as a way of remembering different events or people. They usually recorded births and deaths in the family Bible. There were no official records kept. They may also have keepsakes from their homes back East and along their journey. Students will create a pioneer scrapbook of their journey through pioneer times. Students will be introduced to the idea of scrapbooks. What might you find in them? What would be important to keep? What would be fun to keep? They will also be introduced to record keeping on the frontier, diary writing and how to keep a travel log.

Students will construct a scrapbook that covers their journey through this unit. They can work in groups and each member can be responsible for a different portion of the scrapbook.

The scrapbook should include:

- Title/illustrated cover

- Table of contents

- Family tree

- Description of your previous home

- List of family members who were on the journey

- Supply list

- Travel log – talk about how you traveled and the length of your journey

- Diary entries from different family members

- Description of people who you met along the way

- If desired, students can draw maps and pictures of important people and places along the way.

Students will present an organized scrapbook that includes all required information. The diary entries will be appropriate to the time period of the frontier. Extra credit can be given to students who include maps and illustrations. See Handout #3: *Pioneer Rubric*.

Handout #3: Pioneer Rubric

Name:_____

Category	Excellent	Good	Satisfactory	Needs Improvement
Required Elements	Scrapbook includes all required elements as well as a few additional elements.	Scrapbook includes all required elements and one additional element.	Scrapbook includes all required elements.	One or more required elements were missing from the scrapbook
Spelling & Grammar	No spelling or grammatical mistakes in a scrapbook with large amounts of text.	No spelling or grammatical mistakes in a scrapbook with little text.	One spelling or grammatical error in the scrapbook.	Several spelling and/or grammatical errors in the scrapbook.
Clarity and Neatness	Scrapbook is easy to read and all elements are clearly written, labeled, or drawn.	Scrapbook is easy to read and most elements are clearly written, labeled, or drawn.	Scrapbook is hard to read with rough drawings and labels.	Scrapbook is hard to read and navigate. It would be impossible for another person to understand the presentation without asking lots of questions.
Use of Time	Uses time well during each class period (as addressed via teacher observation) with no adult reminders.	Uses time well during most class periods (as assessed via teacher observation) with no adult reminders.	Uses time well (as assessed via teacher observation), but required adult reminders on one or more occasions.	Uses time poorly (as assessed via teacher observation) in spite of several adult reminders to do so.
Cooperation	Works cooperatively with partner at all times with no need for adult supervision.	Works cooperatively with partner most of the time but had a few problems that the team resolves themselves.	Works cooperatively with partner most of the time, but has one problem that required adult intervention.	Works cooperatively with partners some of the time, but has several problems that required adult intervention.

Immigration

Introduction:

Where did your family come from? I don't mean Boston or Chicago, but where else? Most Americans can trace their roots back to another country. There are Irish Americans, French Americans, African Americans, Polish Americans, and Native Americans. Very few consider themselves "Americans." In this chapter we will be reading about the lives of characters who left their homeland and moved to America. Most were in search of a better lifestyle, some were interested in religious freedom, some were seeking economic freedom, and some came to America against their will. This topic lends itself nicely to many classroom projects and discussions. Have a great journey with your students through this unit.

Standards Addressed (McREL)
United States History
Era 4 – Expansion and Reform (1801–1861)

Standard 10
Understands how the industrial revolution, increasing immigration, the rapid expansion of slavery, and the westward movement changed American lives and led to regional tensions

Level II Grade: 5–6

1. Understands the lives of immigrants in American society during the antebellum period (e.g., factors that led to increased immigration from China, Ireland, and Germany; how immigrants adapted to life in the United States and to hostility from the nativist movement and the "Know-Nothing" party)

3. Understands social and economic elements of urban and rural life in the early and mid-19th centuries (e.g., the impact of the factory system on gender roles and the daily life of men, women, and children; factors that caused rapid urbanization; city life in the 1840s; differences in urban and rural children's lives, life in New England mill towns in the early 1800s, the impact of the canal and railroad on the locations and size of cities after 1820)

5. Understands how slavery shaped social and economic life in the South after 1800 (e.g., how the cotton gin and the opening of new lands in the South and West led to increased demands for slaves; differences in the lives of plantation owners, poor free black and white families, and slaves; methods of passive and active resistance to slavery; escaped slaves and the Underground Railroad)

Era 6 – The Development of the Industrial United States (1870–1900)

Standard 17
Understands massive immigration after 1870 and how new social patterns, conflicts, and ideas of national unity developed amid growing cultural diversity

Level II Grade: 5-6

1. Understands patterns of immigrant life after 1870 (e.g., where people came from and where they settled; how immigrants formed a new American culture; the challenges, opportunities, and contributions of different immigrant groups; ways in which immigrants learned to live and work in a new country)

Standards Addressed (NETS)
Performance Indicators For Technology-Literate Students

Grades 3-5

4. Use general purpose productivity tools and peripherals to support personal productivity, remediate skill deficits, and facilitate learning throughout the curriculum.

5. Use technology tools (e.g., multimedia authoring, presentation, Web tools, digital cameras, scanners) for individual and collaborative writing, communication, and publishing activities to create knowledge products for audiences inside and outside the classroom.

6. Use telecommunications efficiently to access remote information, communicate with others in support of direct and independent learning, and pursue personal interests.

Sample Booktalk:

Nixon, Joan Lowery. *Land Of Hope*. Milwaukee, WI: G. Stevens, 2001, c1992, IL 3-6, RL 5.2

Rebekah's life is about to change forever. But will it be for the better? Her family will be emigrating from Russia to the United States. Life in Russia in 1902 is not a safe place for Jews. Rebekah's father has made the difficult decision to take his family to join his brother in New York City. There are opportunities to make a good living and there is the hope of religious freedom there. When they board the ship that will take them on their journey, Rebekah is dismayed at the horrible conditions the family will endure for the next two weeks. What makes the journey bearable is finding two other girls who are near her age and also beginning a new life in America. Kristin Swenson is from Sweden and Rose Carney is from Ireland. Kristen tells Rebekah about the opportunities America holds for them. It is even possible for a girl to get an education, which has been Rebekah's dream for a long time. She can't believe she may be able to achieve this dream that would not have been possible back in Russia. The three girls become fast friends but when they reach Ellis Island, Rebekah faces having to say more goodbyes. Find out what awaits Rebekah in New York in LAND OF HOPE.

Booklist:

Cohen, Barbara. *Molly's Pilgrim*. New York: Lothrop, Lee & Shepard Books, 1998, IL 3-6, RL 2.8
Told to make a Pilgrim doll for the Thanksgiving display at school, Molly is embarrassed when her mother tries to help her out by creating a doll dressed as she herself was dressed before leaving Russia to seek religious freedom.

Hesse, Karen. *Letters From Rifka*. New York: H. Holt, c1992, IL 3-6, RL 5.1
In letters to her cousin, a young Jewish girl chronicles her family's flight from Russia in 1919 and her own experiences when she must be left in Belgium for a time while the others emigrate to America.

Hest, Amy. *When Jessie Came Across The Sea*. Cambridge, MA: Candlewick Press, 1997, IL 3-6, RL 3.5
A 13-year-old Jewish orphan reluctantly leaves her grandmother and immigrates to New York City, where she works for three years sewing lace and earning money to bring Grandmother to the United States, too.

Mayerson, Evelyn Wilde. *The Cat Who Escaped From Steerage: A Bubbemeiser.* New York: Atheneum Books for Young Readers, c1990, IL 3-6, RL 5.4
Living in the steerage section of a steamship bound for America, Chanah tries to keep her newly found cat a secret.

Moss, Marissa. *Hannah's Journal: The Story Of An Immigrant Girl.* San Diego: Harcourt, Inc, c2000, IL 3-6, RL 4.3
In the Russian shtetl where she and her family live, Hannah is given a diary for her 10th birthday, and in it she records the dramatic story of her journey to America.

Nixon, Joan Lowery. *Land Of Dreams.* Milwaukee, WI: G. Stevens, 2001, IL 3-6, RL 5.0
In 1902, 16-year-old Kristin travels with her family from Sweden to a new life in Minnesota. Here she finds herself frustrated by the restrictions placed on what girls of her age are expected or allowed to do.

Ross, Lillian Hammer. *Sarah, Also Known As Hannah.* Morton Grove, Ill.: A. Whitman, c1994, RL 4.5
When 12-year-old Sarah leaves the Ukraine for America in her sister's place, she must use her sister's passport and her sister's name, Hannah.

Tolliver, Ruby C. *Sarita, Be Brave.* Austin, Tex: Eakin Press, c1999, IL 3-6, RL 5.7
When political unrest in Honduras forces 12-year-old Sara to flee with her family and make the dangerous journey north to Texas, she faces the challenges of starting a new school and a new life.

Wilson, Laura. *How I Survived The Irish Famine: The Journal Of Mary O'Flynn.* New York: HarperCollins, 2001, IL 3-6, RL 5.1
In 1847, during the Great Potato Famine, 12-year-old Mary O'Flynn keeps a journal of life and death among Ireland's tenant farmers.

Woodruff, Elvira. *The Orphan Of Ellis Island: A Time-Travel Adventure.* New York: Scholastic, 1997, IL 3-6, RL 5.5
During a school trip to Ellis Island, Dominick Avaro, a 10-year-old foster child, travels back in time to 1908 Italy and accompanies two young immigrants to America.

Suggested Activities:

Activity #1: Immigrant Letters Home

You are an immigrant who has landed in New York City in the year 1900. Write a letter back home to those you've left behind. Tell them what your life is like now and compare it to life back home.

Activity #2: Me Museum

Have students create a "Me Museum" of their ancestors. Have them collect artifacts in a shoebox that represent different ancestors and customs. Present the Museum orally to the class explaining what the artifacts represent.

Activity #3: Passports

Talk to students about travel restrictions between countries. Many would-be immigrants can't come to the United States because they don't have the proper paper work. Explain the use of passports for inter-country travel. Students will then create their own student passports. For one day, have the teacher (or students assigned as passport control) use stamps every time the students pass to a different room in school.

Activity #4: **The Changing Face of Immigration**

The United States is a land of immigrants. Most citizens consider themselves having come from elsewhere. There are Irish-Americans, Asian-Americans, African-Americans, German-Americans, and even Native Americans. Few people describe themselves just as American. In this activity, students will examine the tide of immigration and the reasons behind it.

- Students will learn about the changing tide of immigration.

- Students will understand some of the reasons for immigration.

- Students will become familiar with finding immigration data on the Internet.

- Students will visit http://www.historychannel.com.

- Students will locate the top 10 populations of people who immigrated to the United States and were processed through Ellis Island during the early 1900s.

- Using an outline map of Europe, students will locate and color in the countries represented with most immigrants.

- Students will visit http://www.ins.usdoj.gov/.

- Students will find the top 10 populations of people who immigrate to the United States today.

- Using an outline map of the world, students can locate and color in the countries represented with most immigrants.

- Students will look at the two maps and compare and contrast. How are they similar? How are they different? What accounts for the differences?

- Students should be prepared to discuss and defend their insights.

Activity #5: **Family Tree**

Have students research their family for a family tree. Ask relatives to try to go back at least three generations. Create a family tree. See Handout #4: *Family Tree*

My Family Tree

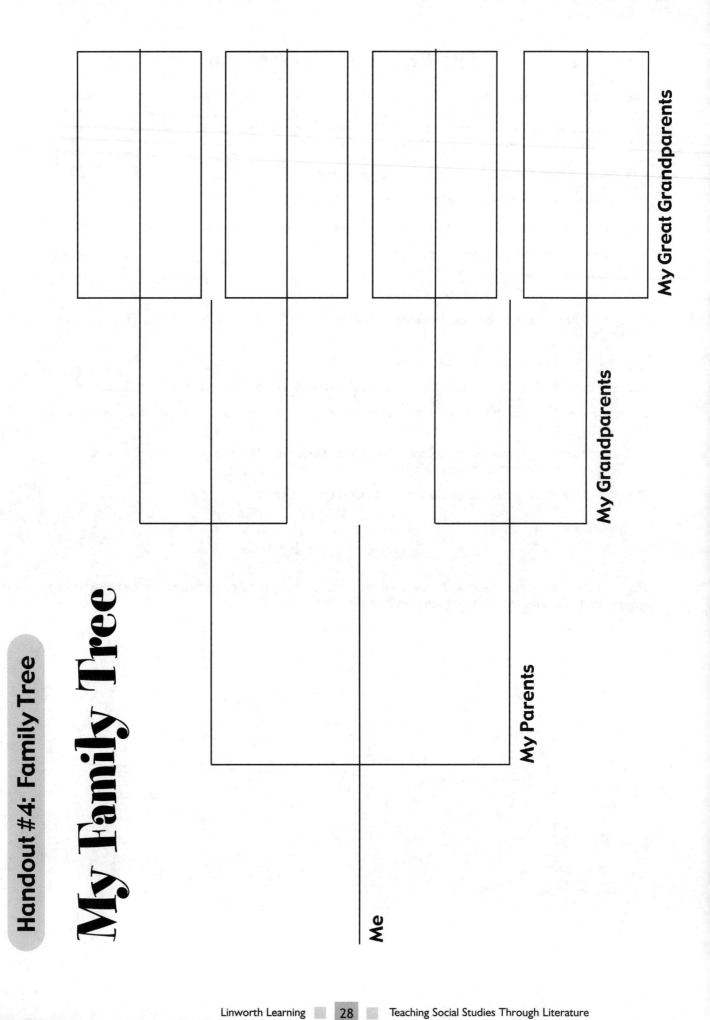

Me

My Parents

My Grandparents

My Great Grandparents

Industrial Revolution/ ❖ Child Labor ❖

Introduction:

It was not unusual for children to help their parents on the farm and in the field. During the 18th and 19th centuries, jobs created in mills were filled by very young children. These children did not go to school and were forced to work long hours. It wasn't until the 20th century that child labor was abolished in many countries. Although it still occurs today, many countries around the world strictly regulate the conditions under which children can work. In this chapter, we will learn the stories of children who did work in factories and under horrible situations. We will look at what their life was like and learn about child labor today.

Standards Addressed (McREL)
World History
Era 7 – An Age of Revolutions, 1750–1914

Standard 33
Understands the causes and consequences of the agricultural and industrial revolutions from 1700 to 1850

Level II Grade: 5-6

1. Understands the emergence and impact of industrialism in 18th-century England (e.g., the effects of the agricultural revolution on population growth, industrialization, and patterns of land-holding; major characteristics of industrialization; how the industrial revolution affected population shifts; how the industrial revolution in the textile industry changed the way people worked; how figures such as John Kay, James Hargreaves, James Watt, Edmund Cartwright, and Richard Arkwright contributed to industrialization in England)

2. Understands the impact of the industrial revolution in Europe and the Atlantic Basin (e.g., connections between population growth, industrialization, and urbanization; the quality of life in early 19-century cities; the effects of urbanization on the development of class distinctions, family life, and the daily working lives of men, women, and children; advances made in communication and transportation; effects upon the political and economic status of women)

3. Understands aspects of the abolition movement in the 18th and 19th centuries (e.g., the organization and arguments of movements in Europe and the Americas that sought to end slavery, and how the trans-Atlantic slave trade was suppressed; why and how the slave trade continued after it had been outlawed; major accomplishments of the American abolitionist Frederick Douglass)

United States History
Era 6 – The Development of the Industrial United States (1870–1900)

Standard 18
Understands the rise of the American labor movement and how political issues reflected social and economic changes

Level II Grade: 5-6

1. Understands changes in business and labor practices during the late 19th century (e.g., reasons for child labor and it consequences, changes in business operation, how workers lives were affected after the Civil War)

Standards Addressed (NETS)

Performance Indicators For Technology-Literate Students

Grades 3-5

4. Use general purpose productivity tools and peripherals to support personal productivity, remediate skill deficits, and facilitate learning throughout the curriculum.

5. Use technology tools (e.g., multimedia authoring, presentation, Web tools, digital cameras, scanners) for individual and collaborative writing, communication, and publishing activities to create knowledge products for audiences inside and outside the classroom.

6. Use telecommunications efficiently to access remote information, communicate with others in support of direct and independent learning, and pursue personal interests.

Sample Booktalk:

Howard, Ellen. *The Gate In The Wall*. New York: Atheneum Books for Young Readers, c1999, IL 3-6, RL 7.0

Ten-year-old Emma can't believe her bad luck! She was a minute late for her job at the silk factory and the owner locked her out. What is she to do now? Her sister is depending on her wages to feed Emma and Nancy's family. When she leans against the wall near the factory, she sees something she has never noticed before. There is a gate in the wall and today it is open. Since she has nowhere to go but back to the depressing room she shares with Nancy, her abusive husband, and their baby, Emma decides to take a look at the world beyond the wall. To her amazement, she finds a quiet, peaceful place. There is a strange boat tied up along what looks to be a small river. When Emma investigates the boat, she finds it is loaded with potatoes. She has not eaten today and quickly takes a potato and hides in a bush to eat it. Even though she has been taught not to steal, she can't help but think about taking a few potatoes to make up for her lost wages. What she can't know at that moment is how drastically her life is about to change. Caught stealing, Emma agrees to work for the boat's owner, Mrs. Minshull, helping get the boat through the narrow canal locks along the river. The life of the boat people is very different from what she has known. She comes to love the life along the locks and even becomes fond of Mrs. Minshull who is hard to like. But Emma can't shake the feeling Nancy and her family need her more than Mrs. Minshull. She feels guilty about being gone so long. Find out what life was like for boat hufflers in 19th century England and what awaits Emma as she journeys through THE GATE IN THE WALL.

Booklist:

Bader, Bonnie, 1961- *East Side Story*. New York: Silver Moon/August House, c1993, IL 3-6, RL 4.3
A young girl and her older sister, working in the Triangle Shirtwaist factory, an early twentieth-century sweatshop on the Lower East Side of New York City, join a protest to try to improve the miserable working conditions.

Collins, Mary, 1961- *The Industrial Revolution*. New York: Children's Press, c2000, IL 3-6, RL 5.9
This book contains a history of the Industrial Revolution focusing primarily on the United States during the nineteenth century and on the change from an agrarian society to one based on machines and factories.

Denenberg, Barry. *So Far From Home: The Diary Of Mary Driscoll, An Irish Mill Girl.* New York: Scholastic, 1997, IL 5-8, RL 3.5.
In the diary account of her journey from Ireland in 1847 and of her work in a mill in Lowell, Massachusetts, 14-year-old Mary reveals a great longing for her family.

Freedman, Russell. *Kids At Work: Lewis Hine And The Crusade Against Child Labor.* New York: Clarion Books, c1994, IL 5-8, RL 6.0
Text and accompanying photographs show the use of children as industrial workers, interwoven with the story of Lewis W. Hine who took these photographs and whose life's work made significant difference in the lives of others.

Kroll, Steven. *When I Dream Of Heaven: Angelina's Story.* Lincolnwood, Ill.: Jamestown Publishers, c2000, IL 5-8, RL 6.8
Angelina Petrosino dreams of getting an education, but her parents insist she work full-time at the Sidowski sweatshop in New York City.

McCully, Emily Arnold. *The Bobbin Girl.* New York: Dial Books for Young Readers, c1996, IL 3-6, RL 3.9
A ten-year-old bobbin girl working in a textile mill in Lowell, Massachusetts in the 1830's, must make a difficult decision—whether or not she will participate in the first workers' strike in Lowell.

Nixon, Joan Lowery. *Land of Hope.* Milwaukee, WI: G. Stevens, 2001, c1992, IL 3-6, RL 5.2
Rebekah, a fifteen-year-old Jewish immigrant arriving in New York City in 1902, almost abandons her dream of getting an education when she is forced to work in a sweatshop.

Paterson, Katherine. *Lyddie.* New York: Lodestar Books, c1991, IL 5-8, RL 6.5
Impoverished Vermont farm girl Lyddie Worthen is determined to gain her independence by becoming a factory worker in Lowell, Massachusetts in the 1840's.

Paton, Walsh, Jill, 1937- *A Chance Child.* New York: Farrar, Straus and Giroux, 1991, IL 5-8, RL 8.0
Compelled to search for his half brother, Creep, who some people insist is nonexistent, Christopher locates Parliamentary Papers containing Nathaniel Creep's personal narrative of working conditions during the Industrial Revolution one hundred years earlier.

Williams, Barbara. *Making Waves.* New York: Dial Books, c2000, IL 5-8, RL 6.0
Having survived the sinking of the Titanic in 1912, twelve-year-old Emily lives in Baltimore where she attends school but also encounters child labor, sweatshops, and the struggle of labor unions.

Suggested Activities:

Activity #1: **Voices Against Child Labor**

During the first part of the last century, a movement to end or limit child labor was begun. Have the students role-play a child laborer from a mill testifying before the legislative committee to protest the use of children in factories. The student should be prepared to discuss his/her daily life and working conditions. S/he should also talk about dreams for their future.

Activity #2: **Child Labor**

The states in the United States have very strict laws regarding child labor. The laws restrict the hours and conditions for children to be employed. Research the issue of child labor abuse and the use of children in sweatshops around the world today. Brainstorm ideas of what you can do to help these children. Who can you write to? Perhaps the students can create a petition or letters that can be mailed to someone of influence.

Activity #4: **Photography of Louis Hine**

Give each of the students a copy of a photograph by Louis Hine. They are available from the National Archives http://www.nara.gov/cgi-bin/starfinder/8952/standard.txt Students should study their photograph and develop a story of what that child's daily life might have been like. They should be able to point to the clues they used to come up with their ideas.

Activity #5: **Timeline of Child Labor**

Have students research child labor laws in the United States. Create a timeline documenting the evolution of child labor laws. At what age can a child start working in your state?

Activity #5: **Factory Workers Today**

Although the conditions may be much better today than 100 years ago, factory work is still a viable source of income for immigrants today. Students will learn about modern factory work and understand why immigrants choose to work there. Introduce students to factory work. Why did children perform this work? Why do some people choose to work there? What skills are necessary to work in a factory? What skills are not necessary?

■ Students will research the mills of New England.

■ What immigrant population replaced the New England farm girls in the factories?

■ Who are the immigrants who arrived during the past 10 to 20 years who have replaced the workers in the factories, mill and service jobs?

■ List three reasons why these types of jobs attract immigrants.

✤ Middle Ages ✤

Introduction:

Knights in shining armor. Damsels in distress. Beautiful castles. What images come to your mind when you think about the Middle Ages? Maybe you think of the plague, filthy living conditions, and poverty. Whatever your view of the Middle Ages, this chapter will provide a book to fit the scenario. We will look at rich people, poor people and the differing living conditions. We'll take a trip back in time and travel the roads of medieval Europe.

Standards Addressed (McREL)
World History
Era 5 – Intensified Hemispheric Interactions 1000–1500 CE

Standard 20
Understands the redefinition of European society and culture from 1000 to 1300 CE

Level II Grade : 5-6

1. Understands the significance of developments in medieval English legal and constitutional practice and their importance for modern democratic thought and institutions

3. Understands the influence of Christianity in medieval Europe (e.g., how successful the Christian states were in overthrowing Muslim powers in Central and Southern Iberia, the reasons for and consequences of the European Crusades against Syria and Palestine)

4. Understands the lives of different groups of people in medieval Europe (e.g., life in Jewish communities and what Jews added to the cultural and economic development of Europe; the influence of ideals of chivalry and courtly love on feudal society; how the status of women changed in medieval European life)

5. Understands the significance of the university in medieval Europe (e.g., how universities contributed to literacy, learning, and scientific advancement; why universities were founded in certain parts of Europe; the meaning of the word "university")

7. Understands aspects of the architecture of medieval Europe (e.g., different architectural styles from this period; how some elements may still be seen in local, modern architecture)

Standards Addressed (NETS)
Performance Indicators For Technology-Literate Students

Grades 3-5

4. Use general purpose productivity tools and peripherals to support personal productivity, remediate skill deficits, and facilitate learning throughout the curriculum.

5. Use technology tools (e.g., multimedia authoring, presentation, Web tools, digital cameras, scanners) for individual and collaborative writing, communication, and publishing activities to create knowledge products for audiences inside and outside the classroom.

6. Use telecommunications efficiently to access remote information, communicate with others in support of direct and independent learning, and pursue personal interests.

Sample Booktalk:

De Angeli, Marguerite. *The Door In The Wall*. New York: Doubleday, 1989, c1949, IL 3-6, RL 6.5

Set in 14th-century England, this is the story of Robin. At 10 years old, he is of the age when he can become a page to a royal and that is what his parents have planned for him. After arranging for his travel, his parents both leave for their own assignments. Before he can take his place as a page, Robin is taken ill and is bedridden. His legs feel like logs and will not do as he demands. Here in plague-riddled England, the servants are afraid he has contracted the plague and they run off, leaving him alone and unable to fend for himself. Finally, Brother Luke arrives and takes Robin to the monastery to mend. Things still don't turn out as planned and Robin's life takes a very different twist. Journey through medieval England with Robin and Brother Luke as Robin searches for his DOOR IN THE WALL.

Booklist:

Greer, Gery. *Max And Me And The Time Machine*. New York: HarperTrophy, 1983, IL 3-6, RL 4.7
Steve buys a time machine at a garage sale and takes his friend Max back to the year 1250, where they land in the middle of a jousting match, with the fierce Sir Bevis as an enemy.

Kirwan, Anna. *Juliet: Midsummer At Greenchapel, England, 1340*. New York: Aladdin Paperbacks, c1997, IL 3-6, RL 7.5
On the day before Midsummer Eve in England in 1340, 11-year-old Juliet accompanies Gil on a trip to obtain medicine for a wounded falcon while hoping to arrive home in time for the fun.

Laksy, Kathryn. *Elizabeth I, Red Rose Of The House Of Tudor (The Royal Diaries)*. New York: Scholastic, 1999. IL 5-8, RL 4.8.
In a series of diary entries, Princess Elizabeth, the eleven-year-old daughter of King Henry VIII, celebrates holidays and birthdays, relives her mother's execution, revels in her studies, and agonizes over her father's health.

Morris, Gerald. *The Squire's Tale*. Boston: Houghton Mifflin, 1998, IL 5-8, RL 5.5
In medieval England, 14-year-old Terence finds his tranquil existence suddenly changed when he becomes the squire of the young Gawain of Orkney. He accompanies him on a long quest, proving Gawain's worth as a knight and revealing an important secret about his own true identity.

O'Brien, Patrick, 1960- *The Making Of A Knight: How Sir James Earned His Armor*.
Watertown, MA : Charlesbridge, c1998, IL 3-6, RL 5.8
Trace James's journey during the Middle Ages in England from inexperienced page at the age of seven to knighthood at the age of 21.

Paterson, Katherine. *Parzival: The Quest Of The Grail Knight*. New York: Lodestar Books, c1998, IL 5-4, RL 5.2
A retelling of the Arthurian legend in which Parzival, unaware of his noble birth, comes of age through his quest for the Holy Grail.

Platt, Richard. *Castle Diary: The Journal Of Tobias Burgess, Page*. Cambridge, Mass.: Candlewick Press, 1999, IL 5-8, RL 6.2
As a page in his uncle's castle in 13th-century England, 11-year-old Tobias records his experiences in his journal while learning how to hunt, play games of skill, and behave in noble society. The book includes notes on noblemen, castles, and feudalism.

Quindlen, Anna. *Happily Ever After*. New York: Puffin, 1999, c1997, IL 3-6, RL 5.2
When a girl who loves to read fairy tales is transported back to medieval times, she finds the life of a princess in a castle is less fun than she imagined.

Scott, Deborah. *The California Kid Fights Back.* New York: Avon Books, c1998, IL 3-6, RL 4.0
When Flattop Kincaid returns to the Middle Ages, he discovers that his friend William has been knighted and he is horrified at Lord Wickshire's cruel treatment of his wife.

Vining, Elizabeth Gray. *Adam Of The Road.* New York: Viking, c1970, c1942, IL 5-8, RL 6.1
Join the adventures of an 11-year-old boy in 13th century England as he searches for his father and his dog.

Suggested Activities:

Activity #1: Knights in Training

Have the students research the stages in a knight's training. Have them describe the attributes of each stage from page to knight. What was life like for each? What must the knights-in-training accomplish to reach the next stage?

Activity #2: Life in a Medieval Castle

Have students research life in a medieval castle. Have them write a "rap" song about the day-to-day life. This song can be written or performed.

Activity #3: A Day in the Life

Assign each student a role of a person from the Middle Ages—e.g. knight, merchant, begger, tradesman, and monk. The student should then research the daily life of this type of person. Students will create a diary for that person, giving insights to daily life and work.

Activity #4: Museum of the Middle Ages

Have students create a Museum of the Middle Ages. Students will create "artifacts" from this time period. Some items found in the museum might include crafts, herbals, armor, etc.

Activity #5: Life in the Middle Ages

Introduction:

Students come to the study of the Middle Ages with some prior knowledge of this time period. However, this may or may not be accurate knowledge. We will look at what they know, what they want to know, and what they learn. Students will use the KWL format.

- Students will brainstorm what they know about the Middle Ages. This will be transcribed on a chart paper titled "What I Know." This will remain posted in the classroom so that students can refer to it.

- Students will then brainstorm ideas of what they would like to know more about. These ideas will be recorded on chart paper and titled "What I Want to Know."

- Students will read a book dealing with the middle ages either individually or as a class.

- After reading the book, students will tell what they learned by reading the material. The third chart will be titled "What I Learned."

- Students will then compare their prior knowledge with their current knowledge. They will also look at their list of things they wanted to know. Have they learned what they want to know? Where can they find more information?

❖ Native Americans ❖

Introduction:

Many of the residents of the United States consider themselves immigrants from other countries. The people who were here when the others started arriving are the Native Americans. The stories about the Native Americans are fascinating ones, and students are drawn to them. In this chapter, we look at some novels about Native Americans, past and present, and have the children extend their knowledge through classroom activities.

Standards Addressed (McREL)
United States History
Era 1 – Three Worlds Meet (Beginnings to 1620)

Standard 1
Understands the characteristics of societies in the Americas, Western Europe, and Western Africa that increasingly interacted after 1450

Level II Grade: 5-6

2. Understands the significance of beliefs held by both Native Americans and Europeans (e.g., Native American beliefs about their origins in America, ideas of land use held by Native Americans and Europeans)

Era 2 – Colonization and Settlement (1585–1763)

Standard 3
Understands why the Americas attracted Europeans, why they brought enslaved Africans to their colonies and how Europeans struggled for control of North America and the Caribbean

Level II Grade: 5-6

3. Understands peaceful and conflicting interaction between English settlers and Native Americans in the New England, Mid-Atlantic, Chesapeake, and lower South colonies (e.g., how Native American and European societies influenced one another, differing European and Native American views of the land and its use)

Era 3 – Revolution and the New Nation (1754–1820s)

Standard 6
Understands the causes of the American Revolution, the ideas and interests involved in shaping the revolutionary movement, and reasons for the American victory

Level II Grade: 5-6

5. Understands perspectives of and the roles played in the American Revolution by various groups of people (e.g., men, women, white settlers, free and enslaved African-Americans, and Native Americans)

Era 4 – Expansion and Reform (1801–1861)

Standard 9

Understands the United States territorial expansion between 1801 and 1861, and how it affected relations with external powers and Native Americans

Level II Grade : 5–6

4. Understands the impact of territorial expansion on Native American tribes (e.g., the Cherokee, Chickasaw, Choctaw, Creek and Seminole removals, the significance of the Trail of Tears, the original lands held by various tribes of the Southeast and those held in the Old Northwest territory)

Standards Addressed (NETS)

Performance Indicators For Technology-Literate Students

Grades 3–5

4. Use general purpose productivity tools and peripherals to support personal productivity, remediate skill deficits, and facilitate learning throughout the curriculum.

5. Use technology tools (e.g., multimedia authoring, presentation, Web tools, digital cameras, scanners) for individual and collaborative writing, communication, and publishing activities to create knowledge products for audiences inside and outside the classroom.

6. Use telecommunications efficiently to access remote information, communicate with others in support of direct and independent learning, and pursue personal interests.

Sample Booktalk

Clifford, Mary Louise. *When The Great Canoes Came*. Gretna, LA: Pelican, 1993. IL 5-8, RL 7.5 .

Cockacoeske is the queen of the Pamunkey tribe. She tells her people the tale of what life was like when the white man arrived in Virginia. Cockacoeske tells of meetings between the Spaniards and the people of the Powhatan tribe. John Smith, John Rolfe and Pocahontas all play a part in the Native American history. The spread of the "white man's fever" among the Native Americans is told through the tale of two young lovers. Hear the story of the settlement of Virginia told from the perspective of a Native American. Find out what happened WHEN THE GREAT CANOES CAME.

Booklist:

Bird, E. J. *The Rainmakers*. Minneapolis: Carolrhoda, c1993, IL 5-8, R L 4.8
An Anasazi boy living long ago in the cliffs of the American Southwest shares a series of adventures with his pet bear and his best friend during his 11th summer.

Bruchac, Joseph. *Children Of The Longhouse*. New York: Puffin Books, 1998, IL 3-6, RL 4.2
Eleven-year-old Ohkwa'ri and his twin sister must make peace with a hostile gang of older boys in their Mohawk village during the late 1400s.

Bruchac, Joseph. *The Journal Of Jesse Smoke: A Cherokee Boy*. New York: Scholastic, c2001, IL 5-8, RL 7.9
Jesse Smoke, a 16-year-old Cherokee, begins a journal in 1837 to record stories of his people and their difficulties as they face removal along the Trail of Tears. The book includes a historical note giving the details of the removal.

Cornelissen, Cornelia. *Soft Rain: A Story Of The Cherokee Trail Of Tears*. New York: Delacorte Press, c1998, IL 3-6, RL 3.5
Soft Rain, a nine-year-old Cherokee girl, is forced to relocate, along with her family, from North Carolina to the West.

Dorris, Michael. *Guests*. New York: Hyperion Paperbacks for Children, 1996, IL 3-6, RL 5.6
Moss and Trouble, an Algonquin boy and girl, struggle with the problems of growing up in the Massachusetts area during the time of the first Thanksgiving.

Durrant, Lynda. *The Beaded Moccasins: The Story Of Mary Campbell*. New York: Clarion Books, c1998, IL 5-8, RL 4.8
After being captured by a group of Delaware Indians and given to their leader as a replacement for his dead granddaughter, 12-year-old Mary Campbell is forced to travel west with them to Ohio.

Erdrich, Louise. *The Birchbark House* . New York: Hyperion Books for Children, c1999, IL 5-8, RL 5.6
Omakayas, a seven-year-old Native American girl of the Ojibwa tribe, lives through the joys of summer and the perils of winter on an island in Lake Superior in 1847.

Markle, Sandra. *The Fledgling*. Honesdale, Pa.: Boyds Mills Press, 1998, IL 5-8, RL 4.8
Orphaned after the death of her mother, 14-year-old Kate runs away to live with her grandfather, a Cherokee Indian who is trying to stop the poaching of predator birds.

Smith, Cynthia L. *Jingle Dancer*. New York: Morrow Junior Books, c2000, IL 3-6, RL 4.2
Jenna, a member of the Muscogee, or Creek Nation, borrows jingles from the dresses of several friends and relatives so she can perform the jingle dance at the powwow. Also included in this book is a note about the jingle dance tradition and its regalia.

Whelan, Gloria. *Night Of The Full Moon*. New York: Random House, 1996, IL 3-6, RL 4.5
In 1840, Libby, who is living with her family on the Michigan frontier, finds herself inadvertently caught up in the forced evacuation of a group of Potawatomi Indians from their tribal lands.

Suggested Activities:

Activity #1: Native American Words

Many of the words we use each day and many of the names of towns and other geographical areas come from Native American words. Have student create a glossary of words used in the English language that have Native American origins. A list to start with is available here: http://www.zompist.com/indianwd.html

Activity #2: Navajo Code Talkers

During World War II, the United States government used native-speaking Navajo tribesmen to pass along secret messages. The Navajo language was hard to decipher which made for a very secure delivery system. These Navajo "code talkers" were extremely important in the war effort. Have students research these men and have fun using a Navajo code takers' dictionary to create their own secret messages. This can be found on the U.S. Navy's website: http://www.history.navy.mil/faqs/faq61-4.htm

Activity #3: Demographic Data

Where do Native Americans live today? Using demographic data taken from the US Census site (http://www.census.gov/), have students create a map showing where Native Americans are living today? Is there a pattern? If so, what may contribute to that?

Activity #4: **Native American Hypertext Essay**

When the Europeans arrived in North America, they found there were others already living in the area. The Native Americans were here long before the Europeans. They had different customs and beliefs which often led to conflict. In this activity, students will research the history of one Native American tribe. The students will then write a hypertext essay which will be published on the Internet.

■ Students will become familiar with Native American tribes.

■ Students will learn to use a simple Web page composer such as Netscape Composer.

■ Students will learn to link pages within a Web site.

■ Students will learn to sketch out Web site development.

■ Each student will be assigned a Native American tribe to research.

■ Students will use library print sources, electronic resources and the Internet to gather information.

■ Students will use the Internet to locate appropriate sites that contain information about the tribe.

■ Students will write a short essay about their assigned Native American tribe.

■ Students will include five hot links within their essays that point to other sites. The links will include:

> ▶ Three Internet sites with information to support the essay

> ▶ Two links should be to pages composed by the student. These pages must be appropriate to the essay. Examples of some student-generated pages include: a bibliography of books dealing with the tribe or Native Americans in general; a drawing done by the student ; a poem written by the student, etc.

■ Essays can be uploaded onto the school server or previewed locally from a disk, the hard drive, or the school's server. Remember you need to obtain parental permission before posting any student work on the Internet and do not use student's full names or identifying information on a Web page.

(For examples of hypertext essays, visit http://www.nancykeane.com/sacks)

Activity #5: **Native American Myths**

There are many wonderful legends and myths that come from the Native American cultures. Have students read and act out one of them. See Handout #5: *Native American Legends*

NATIVE AMERICAN LEGENDS

Bruchac, Joseph. *Thirteen Moons On Turtle's Back: A Native American Year Of Moons*. New York: Philomel Books, New York: c1992.

Bruchac, Joseph. *When The Chenoo Howls: Native American Tales Of Terror*. New York: Walker, 1998.

Bruchac, Joseph, *Flying With The Eagle, Racing The Great Bear: Stories From Native North America*. New York: Troll Medallion, c1993.

Bruchac, Joseph. *The Earth Under Sky Bear's Feet: Native American Poems Of The Land*. New York: Putnam & Grosset, 1998, c1995.

Bruchac, Joseph. *Return Of The Sun: Native American Tales From The Northeast Woodlands*. Freedom, CA: Crossing Press, c1990.

Caduto, Michael J. *Keepers Of The Night: Native American Stories And Nocturnal Activities For Children*. Golden, CO: Fulcrum Pub., c1994.

Caduto, Michael J. *Keepers Of The Animals: Native American Stories And Wildlife Activities For Children*. Golden, CO: Fulcrum Pub., c1997.

Caduto, Michael J. *Keepers Of The Earth: Native American Stories And Environmental Activities For Children*. Golden, CO: Fulcrum Pub., c1997.

Doherty, Craig A. *The Huron*. Vero Beach, FL: Rourke Publications, c1994.

Hamilton, Virginia. *In The Beginning: Creation Stories From Around The World*. San Diego: Harcourt Brace Jovanovich, c1988.

Monroe, Jean Guard. *They Dance In The Sky: Native American Star*. Boston: Houghton Mifflin, c1987.

Press, Petra. *Indians Of The Northwest: Traditions, History, Legends, And Life*. Milwaukee WI: Gareth Stevens Pub., c2000.

Sita, Lisa. *Indians Of The Great Plains: Traditions, History, Legends, And Life*. Milwaukee WI: Gareth Stevens Pub., c2000.

Sita, Lisa. *Indians Of The Northeast: Traditions, History, Legends, And Life*. Milwaukee WI: Gareth Stevens Pub.,

Sita, Lisa. *Indians Of The Southwest: Traditions, History, Legends, And Life*. Milwaukee WI: Gareth Stevens Pub.,

Taylor, C. J. (Carrie J.). *How We Saw The World: Nine Native Stories Of The Way Things Began*. Plattsburgh, NY.: Tundra Books, c1993.

Vogel, Carole Garbuny. *Legends Of Landforms: Native American Lore And The Geology Of The Land*. Brookfield, CT: Millbrook Press, c1999.

Vogel, Carole Garbuny. *Weather Legends :—Native American Lore And The Science Of Weather*. Brookfield, CT: Millbrook Press, c2001.

Williamson, Ray A. *First Houses: Native American Homes And Sacred Structures*. Boston: Houghton Mifflin, c1993.

Wood, Marion. *Myths And Civilization Of The Native Americans*. New York: Peter Bedrick Books, c1998.

❖ Pirates ❖

Introduction:

Arrgh, maties! Are ye ready to walk the plank? How about taking a journey to a new place and finding all the riches you can imagine? How about looting a ship bound for the new world loaded with treasure? We may need to bury our treasure on a remote island so others can't find it. Remember to draw a map so we can find it again when the coast is clear! Whatever you do, don't tell the parrot a thing. He can't keep his mouth shut and always squawking our business around! Let's get to the loot!

Standards Addressed (McREL)
United States History

Standard 2
Understands cultural and ecological interactions among previously unconnected people resulting from early European exploration and colonization

Level II Grade: 5-6

1. Knows the features of the major European explorations that took place between the 15th and 17th centuries (e.g., the routes and motives of Spanish, French, Dutch, and English explorers; the goals and achievements of major expeditions; problems encountered on the high seas; fears and superstitions of the times; what sailors expected to find when they reached their destinations)

World History
Era 4 - Expanding Zones of Exchange and Encounter, 300-1000 CE

Standard 15
Understands the political, social, and cultural redefinitions in Europe from 500 to 1000 CE

Level II Grade: 5-6

3. Understands the significance of Norse migrations and invasions (e.g., how Norse explorations stimulated the emergence of independent lords and the knightly class; locations of Norse settlements, including routes to North America, Russia, Western Europe, and the Black Sea)

Standard 17
Understands the rise of centers of civilization in Mesoamerica and Andean South America in the 1st millennium CE

Level II Grade: 5-6

1. Understands the significant features of Mayan civilization (e.g., locations of Mayan city-states, road systems, and sea routes in Mesoamerica and the influence of the environment on these developments; the role and status of elite women and men in Mayan society as indicated by their portrayal in Mayan monumental architecture; the importance of religion in Mayan society; the structure and purpose of Mayan pyramids; ceremonial games among the Mayans)

Era 6 – Global Expansion and Encounter, 1450–1770

Standard 26

Understands how the transoceanic interlinking of all major regions of the world between 1450 and 1600 led to global transformations

Level II Grade: 5–6

1. Understands the interregional trading system that linked peoples of Africa, Asia, and Europe on the eve of the European overseas voyages

Standards Addressed (NETS)

Performance Indicators For Technology-Literate Students

Grades 3–5

4. Use general purpose productivity tools and peripherals to support personal productivity, remediate skill deficits, and facilitate learning throughout the curriculum.

5. Use technology tools (e.g., multimedia authoring, presentation, Web tools, digital cameras, scanners) for individual and collaborative writing, communication, and publishing activities to create knowledge products for audiences inside and outside the classroom.

6. Use telecommunications efficiently to access remote information, communicate with others in support of direct and independent learning, and pursue personal interests.

Sample Booktalk:

Gregory, Kristiana. *The Stowaway: a Tale of California Pirates*. New York: Scholastic, 1995. IL 3-6, RL 5.8

Pirates? You must be joking! Carlito and his family live on the coast of Monterey, California in the year 1818. Of course they have heard of pirates, but never thought they would see any. Word comes that a group of pirates is heading their way and will attack soon. Day after day, Carlito and his friends keep a lookout for the pirates. As much as they are aware of how frightened they should be, they are really excited about seeing some real pirates! When the pirates do arrive, it is with a warning to surrender immediately or face the terrible attack of the ships. The residents of Monterey refuse to surrender and the wrath of the pirates is felt. Carlito witnesses the murder of his father and vows vengeance on the pirates. He and his friends try sneak aboard the pirate ship but only Carlito makes it. The others are lost. Now Carlito finds himself in the position as a stowaway on a pirate ship. He knows he can't hide forever but he doesn't want to be killed either. What will happen to poor Carlito? Will he be able to avenge his father's death or will he become just another casualty of the fierce pirates? Find out as we STOWAWAY on a pirate's ship.

Booklist:

Barrie, J. M. (James Matthew), 1860-1937. *Peter Pan*. New York: Puffin Books, London ; 1994, 1911, IL 5-8, RL 5.1
The story of three children who travel to Neverland with Peter Pan, the boy who won't grow up, and have several adventures, including escape from the nasty Captain Hook.

Bulla, Clyde Robert. *Pirate's Promise*. New York: HarperTrophy, 1994, c1986, IL 3-6, RL 4.6
While on his way to America in 1716, an English boy is captured by pirates.

Hausman, Gerald. *Tom Cringle: Battle On The High Seas*. New York: Simon & Schuster Books for Young Readers, c2000, IL 3-6, RL 5.3
After Tom Cringle turns 13, he sets out on a high sea adventure that takes him to Jamaica, where he patrols the waters against pirates.

Hobbs, Will. *Ghost Canoe.* New York: Morrow Junior Books, c1997, IL 5-8, RL 5.5
Fourteen-year-old Nathan, fishing with the Makah in the Pacific Northwest, finds himself holding a vital clue when a mysterious stranger comes to town looking for Spanish treasure.

Hughes, Carol. *Jack Black & The Ship Of Thieves.* New York: Random House, 2000, IL 5-8, RL 6.2
Having fallen from his father's airship, Jack blunders into a feud between a pirate ship and a deadly ocean-going war machine and encounters danger, intrigue, and treachery.

Lehr, Norma. *The Secret Of The Floating Phantom.* Minneapolis: Lerner, c1994, IL 3-6, RL 4.5
While staying with her grandmother in Monterey, California, 11-year-old Kathy has some strange experiences as she is led by a foglike phantom to treasure hidden from pirates more than 150 years ago.

Oliver, Martin. *Agent Arthur On The Stormy Seas.* London: Usborne, 1991, IL 3-6, RL 4.8,
The reader must decipher clues and puzzles to help solve a mystery in which Agent Arthur stumbles onto the secret base of a gang of pirates and must act fast to thwart their evil plans.

Scieszka, Jon. *The Not-So-Jolly-Roger.* New York: Viking, 1991, IL 3-6, RL 5.2
Blackbeard, the meanest pirate who has ever lived, has our accidental time travelers cornered. Should Fred, Sam, and Joe the Time Warp Trio join his pirate crew, or become shark munchies?

Stevenson, Robert Louis, 1850-1894. *Treasure Island.* New York: Grosset & Dunlap, 1994, IL 5-8, RL 7.0
While going through the possessions of a deceased guest who owed them money, the mistress of the inn and her son find a treasure map that leads them to a pirate's fortune.

Yolen, Jane. *The Ballad Of The Pirate Queens.* San Diego: Harcourt Brace, c1995, IL 3-6, RL 6.2
Two women who sailed with Calico Jack Rackham and his pirates in the early 1700s do their best to defend their ship while the men on board are busy having a party.

Suggested Activities:

Activity #1: What Do We Know About Pirates?

Have students complete a quick write-up of what they know about pirates. Have them put their information into two categories of "what they know" and "what they think they know." Compare the information from the class. How many facts has the class brainstormed about pirates? What is the consensus as to which are true or possibly true? Ask students if any of the information should be eliminated from the list because it is untrue.

Activity #2: Pirate Flags

Most pirate ships flew distinctive flags that identified the ship. Have the students design their own individual pirate flag to reflect their personality. These two-sided designs can be hung on the wall, from the suspended ceiling, or on the desks.

Activity #3: Wanted Poster

Pirates were criminals and were often in trouble with the law. Since they sailed from place to place, it was often difficult for a particular government to catch them. Choose a pirate from one of the books you have read and create a "wanted poster" for him/her. Include why the pirate is wanted by the authorities by listing the crimes he/she has committed. Draw a picture of the pirate and list any distinguishing marks such as scars or tattoos. What characteristics of the pirate will make it easy to find him/her? Offer a reward if you want. Include information of who to contact in case the pirate is seen. See Handout #6: *Wanted Poster.*

WANTED BY
Her Royal Majesty

Name:

ALIASES: Suspect uses the following names:

DESCRIPTION:
DOB:
Height:
Weight:
Eye color:
Hair color:
Scars, tattoos or other noticeable markings:

OCCUPATION:

CRIMES:

REWARD:

If spotted, do not attempt to apprehend the suspect. Report sightings to:

**Scotland Yard
London, England**

Activity #4: Postcards From the Sea

Create a pirate postcard. The postcard will be one the pirate may have sent to another pirate. On one side of the paper, draw a scene that the pirate would have seen. This may be an island, a country or anything appropriate. On the other side, address the postcard to another pirate and tell why s/he should visit the place shown.

Activity #5: Finding the Pirate Treasure

In this unit, we have been talking about pirates and the legends of pirates. One of the common items associated with pirates is the infamous treasure map. Pirate lore contends pirates buried their treasures in remote places so they could return when the time was right and it was safe to do so. In this activity, students will practice their map reading skills and following directions. Read various books about pirates. Students will need to be instructed in map reading skills. Using a map of the school, instruct students how to find various parts of the school using the map. Students should also have some skills in following directions.

Materials	Instructions
■ Map of school ■ "Treasure Map" created by teacher. The map should include both written directions and symbols representing areas of the school. For instance, you can use a symbol for the library such as a book. A sample direction might be, "Go to <book symbol>. Facing the door, turn left and walk seven paces." ■ Hide small treats that will serve as the treasure. Chocolate coins in mesh bags make the best treasure.	■ Students will work in groups. The teacher will determine the number of students per group. ■ Each group will be given a map of the school and a "Treasure Map." ■ Students will be reminded about appropriate behavior during the hunt. ■ Students will work together to follow the directions on the map to find the treasure.

✦ Racial Relations ✦

Introduction:

Throughout cultures all around the world, there has always been a history of different races struggling to coexist. Be it racial divisions, religious divisions or something else, people are still trying to learn to live together peacefully. In this chapter, we will examine racial relations in the United States. We will concentrate primarily on the 20th century and the Civil Rights movement of the 1960s. Students will come to understand differences must be overcome in order to live together in harmony.

Standards Addressed (McREL)
United States History
Era 9 – Postwar United States (1945 to early 1970s)

Standard 28
Understands domestic policies in the post-World War II period

Level II Grade: 5-6

1. Understands the civil rights movement during President Truman's presidency (e.g., his support of civil rights, the effect on the Democratic party)

Standard 29
Understands the struggle for racial and gender equality and for the extension of civil liberties

Level II Grade: 5-6

1. Understands the development of the civil rights movement (e.g., the Supreme Court case Brown v. Board of Education and its significance in advancing civil rights; the resistance to civil rights in the South between 1954 and 1965; how the "freedom ride," "civil disobedience," and "non-violent resistance" were important to the civil rights movement; Martin Luther King Jr.'s "I Have a Dream" speech in the context of major events)

2. Understands the involvement of diverse groups in the Civil Rights movement (e.g., the agendas, strategies, and effectiveness of African, Asian, Latino, and Native Americans, as well as the disabled, in advancing the movement for civil and equal rights; regional issues important to diverse groups and their efforts to attain equality and civil rights after World War II)

Standards Addressed (NETS)
Performance Indicators For Technology-Literate Students

Grades 3-5

4. Use general purpose productivity tools and peripherals to support personal productivity, remediate skill deficits, and facilitate learning throughout the curriculum.

5. Use technology tools (e.g., multimedia authoring, presentation, Web tools, digital cameras, scanners) for individual and collaborative writing, communication, and publishing activities to create knowledge products for audiences inside and outside the classroom.

6. Use telecommunications efficiently to access remote information, communicate with others in support of direct and independent learning, and pursue personal interests.

Sample Booktalk:

Davis, Ossie. *Just Like Martin*. New York: Simon & Schuster, 1992. IL 5-8, RL 5.7

Life in their Alabama town is about to change. Fourteen-year-old Isaac Stone is put in charge of planning a church trip to hear Martin Luther King, Jr. speak in Washington, D.C. He is honored he has been chosen to do this. Isaac is a true believer of Dr. King's ideals and tries to be a role model of non-violent behavior for others. Many of the other residents of the town do not agree with Isaac. They feel the only way to deal with each other is through the use of a gun. Even when the other kids make fun of Isaac because of his beliefs, he stays true to his feelings. When Dr. King comes to the town to speak, Isaac's family and friends are so overcome by his words they begin to believe that there may be a change coming. But will this newfound optimism be enough to make changes? Will Isaac's father give up his gun and his racism? Ride along with Isaac as he tries to be JUST LIKE MARTIN.

Booklist:

Armistead, John. *The $66 Summer*. Minneapolis, MN: Milkweed Editions, 2000, IL 5-8, RL 5.9
Thirteen-year-old George, spending the summer of 1955 working in his grandmother's store in Obadiah, Alabama, becomes involved with helping his African-American friends, Esther and Bennett, solve the mystery of their father's disappearance.

Curtis, Christopher Paul. *The Watsons Go To Birmingham—1963: A Novel*. New York: Delacorte Press, c1995, IL 5-8, RL 5.0
The ordinary interactions and everyday routines of the Watsons, an African-American family living in Flint, Michigan, are drastically changed after they go to visit Grandma in Alabama in the summer of 1963.

English, Karen. *Francie*. New York: Farrar Straus Giroux, 1999, IL 5-8, RL 5.0
When the 16-year-old boy whom she tutors in reading is accused of attempting to murder a white man, Francie gets herself in serious trouble for her efforts at friendship.

Hearne, Betsy Gould. *Listening for Leroy*. New York: M.K. McElderry Books, c1998, IL 3-6, RL 5.2
Growing up in rural Alabama in the 1950s, 10-year-old Alice has no one to talk to but Leroy, the black farmhand. When Alice's doctor father moves the family to Tennessee, she has trouble fitting in and she sorely misses Leroy.

Meyer, Carolyn. *White Lilacs* . San Diego: Harcourt Brace Jovanovich, c1993, IL 5-8, RL 5.0
In 1921 in Dillon, Texas, 12-year-old Rose Lee sees trouble threatening her black community when the whites decide to take land for a park and forcibly relocate the black families to an ugly stretch of territory outside the town.

Nelson, Vaunda Micheaux. *Beyond Mayfield*. New York: G.P. Putnam's, c1999, IL 5-8, RL 6.3
In 1961, the children of Mayfield are concerned with air-raid drills and fallout shelters, but the Civil Rights movement becomes real when a neighbor joins the Freedom Riders.

Robinet, Harriette. *Walking To The Bus-Rider Blues*. New York: Atheneum Books for Young Readers, c2000, IL 3-6, RL 4.9
Twelve-year-old Alfa Merryfield, his older sister, and their grandmother, struggle for rent money, food, and their dignity as they participate in the Montgomery, Alabama bus boycott in the summer of 1956.

Taylor, Mildred D. *The Gold Cadillac*. New York: Dial, 1987, IL 3-6, RL 6.0
Two black girls living in the North are proud of their family's beautiful new Cadillac until they take it on a visit to the South and encounter racial prejudice for the first time.

Taylor, Mildred D. *Roll Of Thunder, Hear My Cry.* New York: Phyllis Fogelman Books, 2001, c1976, IL 5-8, RL 6.9
An African-American family living in Mississippi during the Depression of the 1930s is faced with prejudice and discrimination, which the children do not understand.

Young, Ronder Thomas. *Learning By Heart.* Boston: Houghton Mifflin, c1993, IL 5-8, RL 3.9
In the early 1960s, 10-year-old Rachel sees changes in her family and her small Southern town as she tries to sort out how she feels about her young black maid, racial prejudice, and her responsibility for her own life.

Suggested Activities:

Activity #1: **Racism in the United States**

Have the students discuss racism in the United States today. Does it still exist? How is it displayed? Create a list of examples of racial discrimination. What can be done to stop it?

Activity #2: **Civil Rights Movement**

Create a timeline of the civil rights movement. Begin the timeline with the end of the Civil War and bring it up to the current day. Include highlights of the movement and those people who were leaders.

Activity #3: **Martin Luther King, Jr.**

Have students research the life of Martin Luther King, Jr. What were some of his influences? Where there indications during his childhood he was destined for greatness? Children should write a short biography highlighting King's accomplishments.

Activity #4: **Abolitionist Movement**

Have students research the abolitionist movement of the 19th century. Have students learn about Frederick Douglass' role in the early civil rights movement, how Sojourner Truth contributed to the movement, and find out who brought the antislavery settlers to Kansas and how that influenced the civil rights movement.

Activity #5: **Experiencing Discrimination**

There are many different forms of discrimination. No matter where people live or what their community is like, you will find discrimination. Sometimes it is blatant and sometimes much more subtle. In this activity, students will be exposed to seemingly meaningless discrimination.

■ Define discrimination and brainstorm what it might "look" like.

■ Have students brainstorm behavior that can be seen as discrimination.

■ As students enter the classroom, use predetermined criteria to divide them up. Shoe style, blue eyes vs. brown eyes, or color of clothing are good criteria to use.

■ For one group, allow them to enter the classroom as usual. The other group is asked to wait in the hall until all the other students are seated.

■ When all students have arrived, direct the "chosen" students to sit in the front seats for a special treat.

- The students in the hall are told to enter the class but they need to sit on the floor in the back of the room.

- The "chosen" students are told not to interact with those in the back of the room.

- The "chosen" students are given treats while those in the back get nothing.

- After a few minutes, debrief the students and enter a discussion of how it felt to experience discrimination. Both sides should talk about their feelings. See if students can determine what criteria you used to separate the groups.

Vikings

Introduction:

When you think of Vikings, what images come to mind? Viking longboats, great warriors or maybe those hats with the horns on them? The Vikings were Nordic peoples who came from the areas of Denmark, Sweden, and Norway. They traveled throughout Europe raiding and settling large areas of eastern and western Europe during a period of Scandinavian expansion from about 800 to 1100. Their conquests were quite well known throughout the area and they were feared by most. The tales of the Vikings were passed down through the ages via epic sagas. Their legendary raids were the most well known during the dawn of medieval Europe. The tales of their conquests may have been exaggerated so their enemies would fear them even more. In this chapter, we will look at some of the ways Vikings are viewed today.

Standards Addressed (McREL)
World History
Era 4 – Expanding Zones of Exchange and Encounter, 300–1000 CE

Standard 15
Understands the political, social, and cultural redefinitions in Europe from 500 to 1000 CE

Level II Grade: 5-6

3. Understands the significance of Norse migrations and invasions (e.g., how Norse explorations stimulated the emergence of independent lords and the knightly class; locations of Norse settlements, including routes to North America, Russia, Western Europe, and the Black Sea)

Standards Addressed (NETS)

Performance Indicators For Technology-Literate Students

Grades 3-5

4. Use general purpose productivity tools and peripherals to support personal productivity, remediate skill deficits, and facilitate learning throughout the curriculum.

5. Use technology tools (e.g., multimedia authoring, presentation, Web tools, digital cameras, scanners) for individual and collaborative writing, communication, and publishing activities to create knowledge products for audiences inside and outside the classroom.

6. Use telecommunications efficiently to access remote information, communicate with others in support of direct and independent learning, and pursue personal interests.

Sample Booktalk:

Hopkins Andrea ; ill. By Leo Duranona. *Harold the Ruthless: The Saga of the Last Viking Warrior.* New York: Henry Holt and Co, 1996. IL 5-8, RL 6.4

This is a re-telling of the saga of Harald the Ruthless. A saga is a bit like a history book. Before there was the ability to write down history to preserve it, the art of storytelling was used to keep history alive. Many of the most famous Icelandic sagas focused on blood feuds between warring families. Even though Iceland is far away from the Norse kingdoms, most of the surviving sagas are from Iceland because many people fled to Iceland to escape the blood feuds in Norway and Denmark. This saga tells of Harald. Harald lived from 1015 to 1066. He was involved with many bloody battles that were waged to acquire land and wealth. He stopped at nothing to get what he wanted. Once you read about what life was like for the Vikings, you may appreciate your own community a bit more! Find out what life was like during that time in HARALD THE RUTHLESS.

Booklist:

Base, Graeme. *The Discovery of Dragons.* New York: Abrams. 1996. IL 3-6, RL 6.7
A ninth-century Viking, a Chinese girl from the 13th century, and a 19th-century Prussian cartographer recount their dangerous adventures in pursuit of dragons through letters sent home from Europe, Asia, and the jungles of Africa.

Janeway, Elizabeth. *The Vikings.* New York: Random House, c1981, IL 5-8, RL 5.9
An account of the explorations of Eric the Red and his son, Leif Ericson, in the New World, 500 years before Columbus.

Katz, Welwyn Wilton. *Out of the Dark.* New York: Margaret K. McElderry, 1996. IL 5-8, RL 5.3
After he builds and successfully sails the model ship he names after his absent mother, 13-year-old Ben begins to accept his new life in the land of the historical Vikings.

Millard, Anne. *Eric The Red: The Vikings Sail The Atlantic.* Austin, TX.: Raintree Steck-Vaughn, c1994, IL 5-8, RL 6.4
This book describes the life of the Vikings, both at home and abroad, their boat-building and navigational skills, and their connection to England, Vinland, and Russia.

Osborne, Mary Pope. *Viking Ships At Sunrise.* New York: Random House, c1998, IL 3-6, RL 3.2
Their magic tree house takes Jack and Annie back to a monastery in medieval Ireland, where they try to retrieve a lost book while being menaced by Viking raiders.

Philip, Neil. *Odin's Family: Myths Of The Vikings.* New York: Orchard Books, c1996, IL 5-8, RL 5.5
This book retells the myths known by the Vikings, featuring such figures as Odin, Tyr, Thor, and Frigg.

Ross, Stewart. *Find King Alfred!: Alfred the Great and the Danes.* London.: Evans Brothers Limited, 1998, IL 5-8, 6.0
Chronicling the Vikings' winter invasion of Wessex, this book explains how Alfred helped save the Saxon kingdom.

Shetterly, Will. *Thor's Hammer.* New York: Random House, c2000, IL 5-8, RL 6.6
In San Francisco in 1876, three boys from very different backgrounds are rescued from drowning by a magical ship which takes them on a quest to Asgard, home of the Norse gods.

Sutcliff, Rosemary. *Sword Song.* New York: Farrar, Straus and Giroux, 1998, IL 5-8, RL 8.2
At 16, Bjarni is cast out of the Norse settlement in the Angles' Land for an act of oath-breaking and spends five years sailing the west coast of Scotland and witnessing the feuds of the clan chiefs there.

Warner, J. A. *One Norse Town: The Case Of The Suspicious Scrolls.* New York: Learning Triangle Press, c1998, IL 3-6, RL 4.0
The young people in the Kinetic City Super Crew use their high tech skills to determine if a set of scrolls proves their town was founded by Vikings.

Suggested Activities:

Activity #1: **Viking Settlements**

The Vikings traveled far and wide in their quest for land. Using a map of Europe, create a visual representation illustrating where the Vikings settled throughout the area. What was their influence on these areas?

Activity #2: **Vikings in North America**

The Vikings did not stay just in Europe. We know they also traveled to North America. Students can learn more about the Vikings by taking a virtual field trip to the National Museum of Natural History's Viking Exhibition, "Vikings: The North Atlantic Saga." <http://www.mnh.si.edu/vikings/> They should keep a "virtual field trip log," noting interesting facts and information as they proceed. (This site is geared towards older students.)

Activity #3: **Viking Images**

Modern media uses Viking symbols to sell products. We often see Viking images in the media today. Have students collect examples of how Vikings are portrayed in advertisements, comic strips, etc.

Activity #4: **Norse Myths**

The Norse culture included many myths. Read some Norse myths. Students can suggest what they tell us about the life and beliefs of the Vikings. These myths can be compared to the more familiar Greek and Roman myths. Students should note similarities and differences.

Activity #5: **Viking Ornamentation**

The great Viking ships that sailed throughout Europe were decorated with great ornamentation. These ornamental figures represented different gods or animals. In this activity, students will learn about the Viking images and create their own. Show students pictures of the ornamentation that was found on Viking ships. Explain the symbolism behind the ornamentation.

Students will research the ornamentation found on the Viking ships. They will then design their own Viking ship. They should explain what their ornamentation represents.

❖ Index ❖